Pro Jakarta Commons

HARSHAD OAK

Apress™

Pro Jakarta Commons
Copyright ©2004 by Harshad Oak

ISBN (pbk): 1-59059-283-2

Printed and bound in the United States of America 10987654321

Technical Reviewers: Henri Yandell, John Zukowski

Editorial Board: Steve Anglin, Dan Appleman, Gary Cornell, James Cox, Tony Davis, John Franklin, Chris Mills, Steve Rycroft, Dominic Shakeshaft, Julian Skinner, Jim Sumser, Karen Watterson, Gavin Wray, John Zukowski

Assistant Publisher: Grace Wong

Project Manager: Tracy Brown Collins

Copy Manager: Nicole LeClerc

Copy Editor: Kim Wimpsett

Production Manager: Kari Brooks

Production Editor: Janet Vail

Compositor: Kinetic Publishing Services, LLC

Indexer: Valerie Perry

Cover Designer: Kurt Krames

Manufacturing Manager: Tom Debolski

Distributed to the book trade in the United States by Springer-Verlag New York, Inc., 175 Fifth Avenue, New York, NY, 10010 and outside the United States by Springer-Verlag GmbH & Co. KG, Tiergartenstr. 17, 69112 Heidelberg, Germany.

In the United States: phone 1-800-SPRINGER, email orders@springer-ny.com, or visit http://www.springer-ny.com. Outside the United States: fax +49 6221 345229, email orders@springer.de, or visit http://www.springer.de.

For information on translations, please contact Apress directly at 2560 Ninth Street, Suite 219, Berkeley, CA 94710. Phone 510-549-5930, fax 510-549-5939, email info@apress.com, or visit http://www.apress.com.

The source code for this book is available to readers at http://www.apress.com in the Downloads section. You will need to answer questions pertaining to this book in order to successfully download the code.

Contents at a Glance

Contents

Foreword

IN THE FOREWORD to *The Cathedral and the Bazaar* (O'Reilly, 2001), Red Hat Chairman and CEO Bob Young identified two things that must happen if open-source software is going to make a lasting change: Open-source software must become widely used, and the users of the software must communicate and understand the benefits of the software development model.

I think that Jakarta Commons has succeeded on both fronts.

As one of the founders of the Jakarta Commons, I am utterly amazed at the success of the project as it nears the third anniversary of its founding. We knew what we did was going to be useful, but we didn't understand the extent to which the code and the community would grow. There are now 28 released components, 20 in progress in "the Sandbox," and lively, continuous discussion and debate on the mail lists—generally more mail traffic than a person can keep up with. Components have grown and "left the nest"—for example, Jakarta Cactus, the server-side testing framework, began as a Commons component. Most important, community participation has blossomed—from the 10 original committers, we have expanded to 82 as of this writing.

A bit of history: In early 2001, several of us working in various Jakarta subprojects noticed we had a problem. The subprojects had implemented a substantial variety of useful utility packages without any thought of reuse outside of each package's subproject. The result was that subprojects would reimplement (or copy outright) useful utility code from others. More important, we knew we had a trove of software to share but no way for people to find that software and obtain it in a simple and useful package. Driven by the motivation to make that software available and an open community debate on what the solution should be, Jakarta Commons was born—and since has become the place where Java programmers first look for help to solve common problems in server-side and client-side development.

The software is widely used throughout the Java world, both in commercial and open-source software. This familiar set of building blocks helps both developers and users: Developers have well-understood tools to work with, and users are familiar with the configuration and functionality of subsystems such as connection pools when they come from Jakarta Commons.

Equally as important, the growth of the community reflects the continued success of the software development model called *open source*. New components and improvements to existing components are driven by developers and users understanding that they can, to use the standard cliché, "scratch their itch." After showing up, all they need to do is contribute.

To that end, Harshad Oak, in *Pro Jakarta Commons*, brings what some may consider the rarest of contributions to open-source projects: comprehensive documentation. In this book, he covers 16 popular components. In each chapter, you'll find not only background and motivation for the components but, for the working programmer, something even more valuable: code examples. With this book in hand, novice as well as experienced developers will be better able to take advantage of the treasure trove of useful utilities that is Jakarta Commons.

I encourage you to use this book, and the software it describes, to its fullest potential. And then if you have an improvement or an idea for something new, show up at "the Commons" and scratch that itch.

Geir Magnusson, Jr.
Wilton, Connecticut
February 2004

About the Author

 **Harshad Oak** has a master's degree in computer management from Symbiosis, India, and is a Sun Certified Java Programmer and a Sun Certified Web Component Developer. He is the founder of Rightrix Solutions (http://www.rightrix.com/), which is primarily involved in software development and content management services. Harshad has been part of several J2EE projects at i-flex Solutions and Cognizant Technology Solutions. Furthermore, he has written several articles about Java/J2EE for CNET Builder.com (http://www.builder.com/). He is also a guest lecturer on Java and J2EE.

Harshad wrote the book *Oracle JDeveloper 10g: Empowering J2EE Development* (Apress, 2004) and coauthored *Java 2 Enterprise Edition 1.4 Bible* (Wiley & Sons, 2003).

Harshad is passionate about all kinds of writing and has published articles about a wide array of subjects. He is an avid nature lover and enjoys reading nonfiction books. He, however, hopes to soon try his hand at writing fiction and providing some serious competition to the Lords of the Rings and the Harry Potters of the world.

Feel free to send all comments and suggestions to harshad@rightrix.com.

About the Technical Reviewers

Henri Yandell is a Java coder who works by day for Genscape.com and by night for the Apache Software Foundation and osjava.org. He has been a committer to Jakarta Commons and Jakarta Taglibs since August 2001 and involves himself in many parts of the Apache community.

John Zukowski is a freelance writer and strategic Java consultant for JZ Ventures, Inc. His latest endeavor is to create a next-generation mobile-phone platform with SavaJe Technologies. Look for the 1.5 edition of his *Definitive Guide to Swing for Java 2* (Apress, 2004).

Acknowledgments

THERE HAVE BEEN many people involved in this book, each chipping in his/her bit to make this book possible. Thanks, Tracy, for managing the book so well and ensuring that we met schedules while still going through all the processes required for producing a quality book. John and Henri were amazing with their technical reviews and often blew me away with tons of comments, all meant to ensure that the book coverage was proper and that I actually delivered what the reader of such a book would expect. Kim did a great job ensuring the content was smooth and that I did not end up changing the rules of the English language. Thank you, Geir, James, Floyd, Rodney, and Stephen for going through the book and sharing your thoughts about it and its subject. My thanks also go out to Laura, Stacey, and Jackie at StudioB.

My family and friends have been absolutely amazing. Ever since my first book was released, I am being treated like a celebrity. Although Java and technical stuff is all Greek and Latin to most of them, they still keep making valiant attempts to understand what I write and to find a few good things to say about the book. Everyone in the family—including my sister's family, my uncles, my aunts, and my cousins—has showered me with tons of affection. My books have meant that I have spent a lot of time working from my home office lately, and I am probably one of the laziest and yet demanding creatures to have in a house. A big thank you to my father, Baba, for tolerating me and for being as understanding and caring as can be.

Sangeeta has always played a very important role in my books, articles, and other exploits. You are truly wonderful. Thank you so much.

Acknowledgments are quite strange actually because not many of us ever put down into words or convey to our near and dear ones how much they matter. I honestly think everyone should write a short acknowledgment once a year and share it or put it on their blog or their personal home page. I am quite sure that if it was not for the three book acknowledgments I have written so far, I never would have put so much thought into who makes a difference to my existence and why. I also would never have conveyed that to them.

CHAPTER 1

Introducing Jakarta Commons: The Uncommon Commons

IT IS LIKELY THAT you are reading this because you want to do more with less and you believe in working smarter rather than harder. Working smart is the guiding principle for this book; every topic it covers is a smart solution to a specific need. Each topic will make you more effective and efficient, saving you a lot of time and money.

Deciding to adopt new technologies and techniques today boils down to economics. No longer can technology be marketed just on the basis of being the next big thing that is capable of doing fascinating tasks for you. If you want a new technology to be used and to prosper, it has to make economic sense. Adopting Apache Jakarta Commons, apart from the fun involved in using it, makes a lot of economic sense. All software that is part of Jakarta Commons is free and open source.

The Jakarta Commons project Web site is at http://jakarta.apache.org/commons/. From this page, you can easily find links to all the other Commons projects.

The Jakarta Commons project consists of easily reusable components that you can quickly put to good use in any type of Java development. The components are not big applications but sleek little bits of code that do a definite task very well.

The tasks that most of these components undertake are of a general nature, something that many applications might require. Strangely enough, few efforts such as the Commons exist where code is written once and then one piece of well-tested code is reused. I dread to think of how many times the same piece of code to implement something such as connection pooling or to perform simple date formatting operations has been written in the Java world.

It is uncommon to see an effort being made to find a common bit of functionality and to reuse it. Often, even within the same company, people are reluctant to find the code they need and reuse that code. The causes are many; lethargy for finding and understanding somebody else's code and a lack of faith in that code top the list. Another problem is that developers often prefer to copy, paste, and adapt code from an existing application rather than reuse that same piece of code.

1

The key to understanding and using Commons components is knowing when and how to use a particular method or component. As such, the components do not require much understanding of theory or other core fundamentals. In this book, although I delve into the theory behind the need for a particular component and the way it is designed, the focus is on using the components. The book is meant to serve as a ready reference to the components, enabling you to find solutions quickly.

Examining the Apache Factor

Open-source software is becoming mainstream rapidly; however, not everybody is comfortable with the idea of using open-source code. Big businesses do not mind blowing money on software as long as they have someone to hold responsible for it. I have been part of projects in which the client explicitly asked that no open-source software be used apart from anything that comes from Apache.

The Apache name has a big role to play in open-source software. Considering the ubiquitous nature of the Apache HTTP server, Apache is perhaps the biggest name in open source. Apache code has come to be used widely and trusted by everyone in the industry. Therefore, the Apache Jakarta Commons project benefits greatly from the Apache name. The wide acceptance of the Commons components has as much to do with the Apache name as with the quality of the components. Jakarta Commons is a small piece in the overall Jakarta and Apache structure and has a limited and focused scope of operation.

Understanding the Scope of Commons

The charter of any Jakarta project is a good place to learn more about that project. The charter states what the project is meant to achieve and what the scope of the project will be. The Commons charter states, "The subproject shall create and maintain packages written in the Java language, intended for use in server-related development, and designed to be used independently of any larger product or framework."

This conveys what the Commons project is about. The key point is that the components are to be designed in such a way that they exist independently of any larger framework. So most, if not all, components are very small downloads that do not exceed 1 megabyte (MB). Although the charter does say that the components are intended for server-related development, most components are not restricted to server-side development and are quite useful in all kinds of Java development. The Commons charter does not as such put any restrictions on the kind of components that can be part of Commons. So the current set of components cover various functionalities ranging from quickly processing Extensible Markup Language (XML) to database connection pooling.

Getting an Overview of the Components

The Commons project already has more than three dozen components; some have been developed from scratch, and others have been pulled out of bigger projects under Jakarta.

The components that are part of Jakarta Commons are categorized into two parts:

Commons Proper: This section holds components that are in a production-ready state. Experimentation and changes to interfaces will be minimal and systematic with these components. So components in the Commons Proper can be used on projects.

Sandbox: The Sandbox components are those that hold a lot of promise but are still in an incomplete stage. Many of the Sandbox components are still on the drawing board or in beta and alpha releases. Lots of tweaking and experimentation is likely to happen to these components, so using them on live projects is not advisable. Sandbox components, when ready, either can move into the Commons Proper or can be absorbed by some other project.

Software that is still in beta and alpha versions generally does not sit well with most project decision makers. A final release is the least that is expected of open-source projects to even be considered for adoption.

The following are the various components currently featured in the Commons Proper:

BeanUtils: JavaBeans adhering to standard naming conventions as specified in the JavaBeans specification and having private member variables with a public get method to fetch the value of the variable and a set method to set it are often used in Java development. The BeanUtils component greatly simplifies working with these JavaBeans and getting things done while having to write minimal code.

Betwixt: The Betwixt component provides a way to easily convert JavaBeans into XML.

CLI: This component makes working with command line arguments simple and systematic. It provides a methodology to specify arguments, their usage, and access to arguments.

Codec: Codec provides implementations for common encoders and decoders.

Collections: The Collections component goes beyond what is offered by the Java Collections Framework and provides many classes that offer useful collections and utilities. Many collections build on existing core Java Application Programming Interface (API) collections, and others are new creations.

DBCP: The Database Connection Pool (DBCP) component provides the functionality of pooling database connection and optimally utilizing them. Database connections are precious resources that need to be created and used wisely.

DbUtils: The DbUtils component is a handy set of classes capable of easily handling most of the routine tasks that need to be performed while accessing a database using Java Database Connectivity (JDBC).

Digester: Creating, parsing, and using XML files can be quite a pain if only the basic APIs are used. Digester makes working with XML quite simple and is of great use, especially while retrieving information from configuration files.

Discovery: The Discovery component is meant to ease discovery of implementations for various interfaces.

EL: An important addition to Java Server Page (JSP) 2.0 is the support for an expression language. The EL component is an expression language interpreter.

FileUpload: The FileUpload component can provide file upload capability to Web applications.

HttpClient: The HttpClient component goes beyond Hypertext Transfer Protocol (HTTP) features offered by the Net component and provides many features required by a Java client communicating using HTTP.

Jelly: Jelly is a component that can convert XML into executable code. Jelly has many subelements that use the core concept to achieve different ends.

Jexl: Jexl stands for *Java expression language*. The Jexl component provides an expression language engine that implements an extended version of the expression language of JSP Standard Tag Libraries (JSTL).

JXPath: JXPath is an interpreter for XPath. XPath uses simple path expressions to identify nodes in an XML document. You have most likely used XPath to refer to nodes in an XML document while creating an XSL Transformations (XSLT) document. JXPath, however, applies XPath expressions not just to XML but even to objects such as JavaBeans and maps.

Lang: Lang is a component relevant to almost any Java project. The Lang component is like an extension of the core Java API `java.lang` package. The component provides many utility methods to perform basic operations on strings, numbers, and so on.

Latka: Latka is a functional testing tool.

Logging: The Logging component is a simple wrapper over the various logging techniques in use such as Log4J, Java Software Development Kit (JSDK) logging, or just `System.outs`. Using this component is advisable to prevent code being locked into a certain methodology. The logging component can make switching between the various logging techniques a simple task.

Math: Math has been recently promoted to Commons Proper and provides mathematics and statistics features that are not available in `java.lang` or in Commons Lang.

Modeler: The Modeler component is meant to simplify the creation of Model management beans as defined by the Java Management Extensions (JMX).

Net: The Net component is a Java library meant to simplify communication using various protocols such as Telnet, Post Office Protocol 3 (POP3), File Transfer Protocol (FTP), Simple Mail Transfer Protocol (SMTP), and so on.

Pool: Pool is an object pooling API that can also be customized for specific pooling requirements.

Primitives: This component provides collections that can be used with Java primitives. So although you could never have created a `java.util.List` that was a collection of `int` primitives, such things are possible using the primitives component.

Validator: The Validator is a simple framework that provides for defining various validation rules in an XML file. The framework can then enable reuse and consistent application of these rules.

By the time you are reading this, there might be other components that have moved from the Sandbox to the Commons Proper. However, even in the Commons Proper, some components have truly matured and are already being used in many applications while others are not that popular. In the next section, you will look at the kind of Java development that is an ideal candidate for Commons usage.

Where Do You Use Commons?

Commons is useful to any brand of Java development in which you might be involved. It might be Web development using Servlets and JSP or Java Graphical User Interface (GUI) development using Swing. Commons can add a lot of value to your Java development and, most important, make your life easier and your development time shorter. That does not mean that all Commons components are useful to all kinds of applications. Commons components are primarily meant for server-side Java development, and using them in other kinds of development is more incidental.

The nature of the Commons project demands that the components do something specific for a certain need, so most components do just that: They focus on achieving something specific for a certain kind of development. Although using a database connection-pooling component for a Java Swing application that has nothing to do with databases does not make sense, it does make sense for a Web application that is using the database extensively.

So an important part of Commons adoption is that you first pick out components that can offer something useful to the development you have undertaken and then focus all efforts on those components. For instance, I have hardly ever gone beyond using three or four of the components at a time.

Before moving into the technicalities of the Commons packages and what each package does, you should know that the groundwork that has to be done to use all the components is quite similar. All the Commons packages that can boast of a proper release have a binary download available at the official Jakarta binary download site at `http://jakarta.apache.org/site/binindex.cgi`. A binary download is a compressed ZIP or TAR file that does not include any of the source code; as a result, the download file tends to be small.

 TIP *I recommend you also download the source code for the Commons components that you intend to use. In most cases, this involves basic Java code that is quite easily understandable.*

The binary file in most cases will have a name in the format `commons-<ComponentName>-<VersionNumber>.ZIP`. If you have downloaded a TAR version instead of ZIP, the file extension will be `.TAR`.

This file will contain a Java Archive (JAR) file that holds all the class files for that component. The Javadocs also ship as part of the binary download. Not all components provide documentation beyond what is present in the Javadocs. However, the Javadocs are quite extensive and explain each method pretty well. So the best way to understand what a method does is to look at the Javadocs. If that does not suffice, you can always look at the code that actually does the job for you—don't forget you are using open-source software!

To use any of the Commons components, all you now need to do is place the JAR file in a suitable location so that the class loader can easily find the classes in the JAR to be used in your application.

Developing a Web Application

Servlets and JSP-based Web applications have to adhere to a specific directory structure as warranted by the specification. As per the specifications, all Web applications have a directory named WEB-INF that holds the files that are meant to be private and not directly accessible by any clients accessing the application. Within the WEB-INF directory, there are two special directories named classes and lib. The classes directory is where compiled class files are kept during development when these files undergo frequent changes. Any Java 2 Enterprise Edition (J2EE)–compliant server can automatically detect any changes to the classes in this directory and load the newer class file. The classes directory is where, in all probability, you will keep the Java code that is using one or more of the Commons components.

The directory that is more relevant in the context of using Commons is the lib directory. All JAR files containing classes being used by the application are kept in the lib directory. The lib directory normally holds third-party JAR files, such as JDBC drivers or frameworks such as Struts. The Commons JAR files should also be placed into the lib directory, and once done, all other classes in the Web application can use all the classes in the JAR files.

Developing Other Applications

For non-Web applications, you do not have the easy option of using the special features of the WEB-INF/lib directory. You now need to specify the JAR file in the CLASSPATH.

If you are using an Integrated Development Environment (IDE) such as NetBeans, Eclipse, or JDeveloper, you have the option of setting the JAR file location into the CLASSPATH for a particular project or application. You then do not have to edit the CLASSPATH value at a system level. If your IDE of choice provides a feature of *clubbing* many JAR files into a single unit, use that to create a new library of all the JAR files for the various Commons components. I did just that when I began working on this book so that once that library was created, I could associate it with any project I created. Because all components are in distinct packages and some components also have dependencies on other Commons components, this is the best option to get things up and running in no time.

TIP *I am a great believer in using all tools that can make my life easier and make me work as little as possible. So if you are not using any Java IDE yet, choose any one and get going. The learning curve is not at all as steep as you might expect. All IDEs are pretty simple to use once you get the hang of them.*

Why Should You Use Commons?

Many of the features of the core Java API that you use regularly are things for which you could write code. You of course can create new data structures similar to those in the Java Collections API, or you can write something as simple as the trim method of the String class. So why don't you write a trim method specific to your application?

The answer is obvious enough: It makes more sense to use the trim method provided by the String class. No book is complete without quoting this phrase at least once, so I will go ahead and say it: "Why reinvent the wheel?"

You might be wondering what Java API usage has got to do with you using the Commons APIs. The answer is simple: Commons is nothing but Java on steroids. No, those using steroids are not thrown out of the Java Olympics, but instead they are the top contenders to get the gold.

NOTE *Do not expect Commons component methods to have complex logic or calculations. In most cases, the logic involved is pretty simple. However, even 50 lines of simple but well-tested code can be a big asset during development.*

You will now see a simple example to illustrate why you should choose the Commons approach over writing new code. The scenario is that you have to split some text you have received based on a certain separator such as a space or a # symbol and then store the split results in a String array. You would have to use the StringTokenizer class, handle null values, and then store the split contents into an array.

This is not a very difficult case, but it would require about 10 lines of code to be written and, more important, tested and maintained. Would it not be better if you had to write just one line of code and not have to worry about testing the logic or maintaining it?

The Java class is as follows:

```
package com.commonsbook.chap1;
import org.apache.commons.lang.StringUtils;
```

```
public class SplitString {
    public static void main(String[] args) {
        //Split a String into an Array using # as separator.
        String [] splitArr=StringUtils.split("AB#CD#EF#GH", "#");

        for(int i=0; i<splitArr.length; i++ ) {
            System.out.println( i + ") "+ splitArr[i]);
        }
    }
}
```

The only line that provides some action is the line where you call the static split method of the StringUtils class. That is all it will take if you use the StringUtils class that is part of the Commons Lang component and that provides many methods to make fiddling with strings a lot easier.

The output for this example is as follows:

```
0) AB
1) CD
2) EF
3) GH
```

Moving Beyond Jakarta Commons

A few other common components projects have been recently developed that are similar to Jakarta Commons. For example, the Apache DB project has a Commons section at http://db.apache.org/commons/, and the Apache XML project has a Commons section at http://xml.apache.org/commons/. The Apache DB Commons project hosts common components that are related to database development, and the XML project has XML-specific common components.

An Apache Commons project distinct from Jakarta Commons has also emerged at http://commons.apache.org/. Jakarta Commons is meant solely for Java components, and the Apache Commons project is language neutral. Apache Commons is still in its early stages. So, for the time being at least, Jakarta Commons is the only place to look for common Java components.

Summary

The ideal position to use Commons is when your boss pushes you to deliver a project in an extremely short time. Keep things simple, use as many Commons components as relevant, and then tell your boss you had to work really hard and build everything from scratch. A promotion might just follow. It is all about working smart; working hard is just being stupid.

In this chapter, you got a quick overview of Jakarta Commons. In the next chapter, you will explore one of the most popular Commons components, the Lang component.

CHAPTER 2

Using the
Lang Component

IN THE PREVIOUS CHAPTER, I briefly introduced Commons and gave the rationale
for using the various components. In this chapter, you will take on one of the
heavyweights in the Commons Proper, the Lang component.

The Lang component is one of the most popular Commons components. It
was the first component I used, and it is the best way to start off using Commons.
The simplicity and the relevance of Lang to everyday Java problems make the
component useful to Java development of all kinds.

In Chapter 1, you used the StringUtils class in the Lang component to split
a string. If you found that example simple, rest assured that the other functionality provided by the Lang component is just as easy to learn and to use. So if you
are reading this while on a project with the usual tight deadline, do not give yourself an escape route by saying that you do not have time to learn something new.
Invest some time and effort, and your investment will bear fruit, even in the
short term.

In this chapter, you will learn about the various classes in the Lang component
and try out some of the more useful methods provided by each class. Table 2-1 gives
the component details.

Table 2-1. Component Details

Name	Version	Package
Lang	2.0	org.apache.commons.lang

Introducing the Packages Within Lang

The Lang component until version 1 consisted of four packages; however, with
version 2, this number has shot up to six. These packages are as follows:

> **org.apache.commons.lang**: This package provides the classes you are
> likely to use most often while working with the Lang component. The
> package has many utility classes, and each of these provides specific func-
> tionality. These utility classes are what you will focus on in this chapter.

org.apache.commons.lang.builder: The builder package consists of classes that help in creating commonly used methods such as equals, toString, and hashCode that are essential for object comparisons and output generation.

org.apache.commons.lang.enum: This package provides enumerations that are meant to provide the enum functionality that is present in C but is not yet present in Java.

org.apache.commons.lang.exception: This package provides a nested exceptions capability. Nested exceptions were introduced in Java Software Development Kit (JSDK) 1.4 and enable effective tracking of exceptions despite being repeatedly thrown and rethrown.

org.apache.commons.lang.math: This package provides all the number-crunching methods that are commonly required. Although this package is a new addition to version 2, some of the classes, such as NumberRange and NumberUtils, were present in earlier versions in the package org.apache.commons.lang.

org.apache.commons.lang.time: This package is perhaps the best thing that has happened to Lang version 2. Working with Date, Calendar, and SimpleDateFormat ranks very highly on my list of the most annoying things in Java. This package goes a long way in simplifying things.

You will now look at each of these packages in more detail.

Using org.apache.commons.lang

This package consists of the portion of the Lang component that is typically used the most during development. This package has many utility classes consisting of static methods that you could invoke to get a certain task done. The sheer number of classes and methods means that I cannot cover every method. However, I will show the important classes and methods along with examples to highlight their usage.

Because most of the methods and variables you will use are static, you do not have to worry about instantiating the classes and then using and reusing objects. Method invocation in most cases is in the form ClassName.methodName(parameters). The utility classes in the package are in the form XxxUtils where Xxx denotes the class or interface that the utility services. For example, the StringUtils class provides many utility methods that revolve around the class String. These classes should never be instantiated because all their functionality lies in public static methods.

I will now discuss the classes in this package and how to use the various methods.

CharRange

You use the CharRange class to create and maintain a range of characters. The class provides functionality to determine if a character lies in a certain range as well as to determine if one character range lies within another character range. For example, you could create a range from character *d* to character *p* and then check if the character *g* lies in the character range.

CharSet

The CharSet class simplifies creating and using a set of characters. The CharSet can be created from the characters in a string and is especially useful when you want to check if a certain string holds only valid characters. You could create a CharSet and then check each character in the string against the character set.

The CharSet class has two protected constructors, so you can instantiate CharSet only from a subclass of CharSet. However, Lang version 2 has introduced a useful static method named getInstance that can be used to create a CharSet instead of having to extend the CharSet class. Listing 2-1 shows how to create a character set of the vowels *a*, *e*, *i*, *o*, and *u*. You will then use this character set to count the number of vowels in a string.

Listing 2-1. VowelCharSetTrial

```
package com.commonsbook.chap2;
import org.apache.commons.lang.CharSet;

public class VowelCharSetTrial {

    public static void main(String[] args) {
      //Create a new vowel character set
      CharSet vChs = CharSet.getInstance("aeiou");

      String strTest = "The quick brown fox jumps over the lazy dog.";
      int iVowelCnt=0;
      int iTestLen=strTest.length();

      for (int i = 0; i < iTestLen; i++) {

          if(vChs.contains(strTest.charAt(i))) {
            iVowelCnt++; //increment count on a vowel being found
          }
```

```
            }
        System.out.println("String >>" + strTest);
        System.out.println("Number of vowels in the string is "+iVowelCnt);
        }
    }
```

In Listing 2-1, you create a new character set for vowels using the static method getInstance of the CharSet class. The set holds the characters *a, e, i, o,* and *u.* You then use the character set to count the number of vowels in the string The quick brown fox jumps over the lazy dog. This sentence is a special one that uses every letter in the alphabet from A–Z.

Execute the VowelCharSetTrial class without passing any command line arguments to get the following output:

```
String >>The quick brown fox jumps over the lazy dog.
Number of vowels in the string is 11
```

Now that you have seen what a CharSet is, you will move on to a utility class that makes good use of CharSet to provide various character-related utility methods.

CharSetUtils

CharSetUtils provides static methods to handle character-related functionality that is often required during development.

The CharSetUtils class uses the CharSet class discussed earlier to provide the required functionality.

NOTE   *For* CharSet, *case does matter. As a result, the character* b *and the character* B *are not the same.*

Listing 2-2 shows how you use the various methods provided by the CharSetUtils class. In each usage in this example you provide a string and then fiddle with the characters present in the string using CharSetUtils methods.

Listing 2-2. CharSetUtilsTrial

```
package com.commonsbook.chap2;
import org.apache.commons.lang.CharSet;
import org.apache.commons.lang.CharSetUtils;
```

```
public class CharSetUtilsTrial {
    public static void main(String[] args) {
        //Count all occurrences of all the characters specified.
        System.out.println("B and o count = " +
            CharSetUtils.count("BorisBecker", "Bo")); //3
        System.out.println("B,o,k,e and r count = " +
            CharSetUtils.count("BorisBecker", new String[] { "Bo", "ker" })); //8

        //Specified characters deleted.
        System.out.println("Delete B and o = " +
            CharSetUtils.delete("BorisBecker", "Bo")); //risecker
        System.out.println("Delete B,o,k,e and r = " +
            CharSetUtils.delete("BorisBecker", new String[] { "Bo", "ker" })); //isc

        //Keeps only the characters specified
        System.out.println("Keep B and o = " +
            CharSetUtils.keep("BorisBecker", "Bo")); //BoB

        //Removes specified character repetitions
        System.out.println("Squeeze B and o = " +
            CharSetUtils.squeeze("BBooøorisbbbecker", "Bo")); //Borisbbbecker
    }
}
```

In this example, you use the methods count, delete, keep, and squeeze. Upon execution you get the following output:

```
B and o count = 3
B,o,k,e and r count = 8
Delete B and o = risecker
Delete B,o,k,e and r = isc
Keep B and o = BoB
Squeeze B and o = Borisbbbecker
```

Note than even when you pass a string such as Bo, the methods look for the character *B* and *o* and not the string Bo.

Now you will move on to ObjectUtils and see the various features it provides.

ObjectUtils

The ObjectUtils class is a simple one that provides a couple of useful features. The toString method that has been introduced in Lang version 2 can be useful to avoid one of the most deadly problems facing Java developers, the

NullPointerException. You can use the toString method to return an empty string
or a specified string if the String instance provided is null. You could now replace
all ternary operator usages in the form strInstance= (strInstance == null ? ""
: strInstance); with strInstance = ObjectUtils.toString(strInstance);.
Listing 2-3 shows how to use the various ObjectUtils methods.

Listing 2-3. ObjectUtilsTrial

```
package com.commonsbook.chap2;
import org.apache.commons.lang.ObjectUtils;

public class ObjectUtilsTrial {
    public static void main(String[] args) {
        //Create ObjectUtilsTrial instance
        ObjectUtilsTrial one = new ObjectUtilsTrial();
        ObjectUtilsTrial two = one; //Same Reference
        ObjectUtilsTrial three = new ObjectUtilsTrial(); //New Object
        ObjectUtilsTrial four = null;

        //four is null, returns DEFAULT
        System.out.print("1) If null return DEFAULT >>>");
        System.out.println(ObjectUtils.defaultIfNull(four, "DEFAULT"));

        //one and two point to the same object
        System.out.print("2) References to the same object >>>");
        System.out.println(ObjectUtils.equals(one, two));

        //one and three are different objects
        System.out.print("3) Check object references and not values >>>");
        System.out.println(ObjectUtils.equals(one, three));

        //toString method gets called
        System.out.print("4) toSring gets invoked >>>");
        System.out.println(one);

        //Object details displayed..toString is not called
        System.out.print("5) Display object details >>>");
        System.out.println(ObjectUtils.identityToString(one));

        //Pass null get empty string
        System.out.print("6) Pass null and get back an Empty string >>>");
        System.out.println("**" + ObjectUtils.toString(null) + "**");
    }
```

```
    public String toString() {
        return "toString Output";
    }
}
```

The output upon executing this program is as follows:

```
1) If null return DEFAULT >>>DEFAULT
2) References to the same object >>>true
3) Check object references and not values >>>false
4) toSring gets invoked >>>toString Output
5) Display object details >>>com.commonsbook.chap2.ObjectUtilsTrial@5
6) Pass null and get back an Empty string >>>****
```

The defaultIfNull method returns the value DEFAULT because the reference four points to null. Upon finding the null value, the method returns the default value provided. This is a similar functionality to the toString method provided by ObjectUtils; however, in this case you are not restricted to strings.

Next, you use the equals method provided by the ObjectUtils class. Executing this example shows that the equals method compares only object references and that values are not compared.

The identityToString method provides an ingenious way to get the string that is returned when invoking the toString method for any object. The identityToString method returns a string in the form ClassName@HashCode. Note that the hashcode value will vary across machines, so you might get a value other than 5 that is shown in the output. The last line in the output is ****, which shows that an empty string was returned by the toString method.

SerializationUtils

Working with Java Input/Output (I/O) has never been my favorite. Remembering numerous classes, their hierarchies, and when to use what can be quite a pain. You can use the SerializationUtils class to take up the task of serializing and deserializing objects, so you do not have to worry about object input and output streams.

In Listing 2-4, you will serialize a String object to a file and then deserialize the object back from the file.

Listing 2-4. SerializationUtilsTrial

```
package com.commonsbook.chap2;
import org.apache.commons.lang.SerializationUtils;
import java.io.FileInputStream;
import java.io.FileOutputStream;
```

```
public class SerializationUtilsTrial {
    public static void main(String[] args) {
        try {
            //File to serialize object to
            String fileName = "testSerialization.ser";

            //New file output stream for the file
            FileOutputStream fos = new FileOutputStream(fileName);

            //Serialize String
            SerializationUtils.serialize("SERIALIZE THIS", fos);
            fos.close();

            //Open FileInputStream to the file
            FileInputStream fis = new FileInputStream(fileName);

            //Deserialize and cast into String
            String ser = (String) SerializationUtils.deserialize(fis);
            System.out.println(ser);
            fis.close();
        } catch (Exception e) {
            e.printStackTrace();
        }
    }
}
```

Upon executing this code, a new file named testSerialization.ser gets created, the string gets serialized to the file, this string is then deserialized back from the file, and the value SERIALIZE THIS is printed as the output.

The SerializationUtils class also provides methods that can use a byte array to serialize and deserialize. A clone method is also provided that serializes an object to a byte array and then deserializes it back to achieve cloning of the object.

RandomStringUtils

RandomStringUtils is one class that you can have a lot of fun using. The class generates random strings based on various parameters specified. One great option is that you can use it to hold a daily lottery at your desk. The point, of course, is that the source code can be rigged to make you win! A commonly required business application for the RandomStringUtils class is to generate passwords. Listing 2-5 shows some uses of RandomStringUtils.

Listing 2-5. RandomStringUtilsTrial

```
package com.commonsbook.chap2;
import org.apache.commons.lang.RandomStringUtils;

public class RandomStringUtilsTrial {
    public static void main(String[] args) {
        //Random 8 chars string from within the characters ABCDEF
        System.out.print("1) 8 char string using chars ABCDEF >>>");
        System.out.println(RandomStringUtils.random(8, "ABCDEF"));

        //Random 8 chars string where letters are enabled while numbers are not.
        System.out.print("2) 8 char string using letters but no numbers >>>");
        System.out.println(RandomStringUtils.random(8, true, false));

        //Random 8 chars string Alphanumeric
        System.out.print("3) 8 char Alphanumeric string >>>");
        System.out.println(RandomStringUtils.randomAlphanumeric(8));

        //Random 8 chars string Alphabets only
        System.out.print("4) 8 char string -Alphabets only >>>");
        System.out.println(RandomStringUtils.randomAlphabetic(8));

        //Random 8 chars string using only the elements in the array aChars
        //Only charcters between place 0 and 5 in the array can be used.
        //Both letters and numbers are permitted
        System.out.print(
            "5) 8 char string using specific characters in an array >>>");

        char[] aChars = new char[] { 'a', '1', 'c', '2', 'e', 'f', 'g' };
        System.out.println(RandomStringUtils.random(8, 0, 5, true, true, aChars));

        // Begin Lottery code
        System.out.print("6) The two digit lucky number for the day is >>>");
        System.out.println(RandomStringUtils.randomNumeric(2));
        // End Lottery code
    }
}
```

The comments in the code state how you can use various combinations to generate a random string. Use the lottery portion, and you could be soon making a lot of money right at your desk. The output for the previous code running on my machine is as follows:

1) 8 char string using chars ABCDEF >>>FFCAABBA
2) 8 char string using letters but no numbers >>>lKRsjhGg
3) 8 char Alphanumeric string >>>K1ggX460
4) 8 char string -Alphabets only >>>Mlhfvyiv
5) 8 char string using specific characters in an array >>>c2a111a1
6) The two digit lucky number for the day is >>>02

Do not expect to get the same output. In fact, running the same code a second time on my machine generates different output.

StringUtils

StringUtils is the class in the Lang component that provides the most number of static methods to use. StringUtils has methods that can do almost everything you could want to do with a string. The class provides more than 100 methods; you will learn about some of the most useful ones.

The StringUtils class even has some methods such as equals, trim, and substring that do what java.lang.String methods do. The StringUtils methods, however, provide built-in handling for null strings. A string being null is one of the most common causes of NullPointerException being thrown, so using the StringUtils methods is a better option in cases where you might get a null string. The Javadocs for the StringUtils class list all the methods that are null safe. Another useful addition to the Javadocs in Lang 2 is that now every method in StringUtils has some usage examples.

Listing 2-6 shows how to use some of the StringUtils utility methods.

Listing 2-6. StringUtilsTrial

```
package com.commonsbook.chap2;
import org.apache.commons.lang.StringUtils;

public class StringUtilsTrial {
    public static void main(String[] args) {
        //String can be max 12 chars including the ...
        System.out.println("1) Abbreviate Once upon a time >>>" +
            StringUtils.abbreviate("Once upon a time ", 12));

        //Returns index where the Strings start to differ
        System.out.println(
            "2) Index Of Difference between ABCXYZ and ABCPQR >>>" +
            StringUtils.indexOfDifference("ABCXYZ", "ABCPQR"));
```

```java
//Remove the specified string at the end of String
System.out.println("3) Chomp END >>>" +
    StringUtils.chomp("A test String END", "END"));

//Check if string contains only a set of characters. Return boolean
System.out.println("4) Check if 643287460 contains only 0123456789 >>>" +
    StringUtils.containsOnly("643287460", "0123456789"));

//Compare two strings. Case sensitive
System.out.println("5) Compare ABCDEFG and ABCdefg >>>" +
    StringUtils.difference("ABCDEFG", "ABCdefg"));

//Takes Object input and returns empty String if null.
System.out.println("6) Return default string >>>" + "**" +
    StringUtils.defaultString(null) + "**");

//Join all Strings in the Array into a single String, separated by $#$
System.out.println("7) Join Strings using separator >>>" +
    StringUtils.join(new String[] { "AB", "CD", "EF" }, "$#$"));

//SubString
System.out.println("8) Substring >>>" +
    StringUtils.substring("SUBSTRING", 1, 5));

//Reverse a String
System.out.println("9) Reverse >>>" + StringUtils.reverse("REVERSE"));

//No NullPointerException even if null!
System.out.println("10) Trim String. No NullPointerException >>>" +
    StringUtils.trim(null));

//If string is null, empty string returned. Else returns trimmed string
System.out.println("11) Empty String >>>" +
    StringUtils.trimToEmpty(null) + "<<<");

//Compare Strings...No NullPointerException!
System.out.println("12) Comapre null and null >>>" +
    StringUtils.equals(null, null));

//Strip whitespace from start and end of the string.
//If null returns empty string
System.out.println("13) Strip whitespace >>>" +
    StringUtils.stripToEmpty("    ABCD    "));
```

```
                    //Check that a string does not contain any of these characters !@#$%^&*
                    System.out.println("14) Check that ABCD contains none of !@#$%^&* >>>" +
                        StringUtils.containsNone("ABCD", "!@#$%^&*"));
            }
    }
```

Instead of explaining each method in the text, I have placed comments in the code that should explain the usage. Apart from the methods covered in this example, there are overloaded methods with the same name but a different signature. So there is more than one way of using chomp, substring, and so on.

Make it a point to go through what the StringUtils class has to offer before starting to write your own code. Because working with strings is something that has to be done day in and day out, the StringUtils class just on its own is a good enough reason to adopt the Lang component. The output for this example is as follows.

```
1) Abbreviate Once upon a time >>>Once upon...
2) Index Of Difference between ABCXYZ and ABCPQR >>>3
3) Chomp END >>>A test String
4) Check if 643287460 contains only 0123456789 >>>true
5) Compare ABCDEFG and ABCdefg >>>defg
6) Return default string >>>****
7) Join Strings using separator >>>AB$#$CD$#$EF
8) Substring >>>UBST
9) Reverse >>>ESREVER
10) Trim String. No NullPointerException >>>null
11) Empty String >>><<<
12) Comapre null and null >>>true
13) Strip whitespace >>>ABCD
14) Check that ABCD contains none of !@#$%^&* >>>true
```

SystemUtils

SystemUtils is a handy little class that reads the system properties and returns appropriate messages based on the property values. You can use this class to find more information about the host machine and operating system. The most common usage, however, is to check the version of the JSDK being used. So, if you are using the logging introduced in JSDK 1.4, you could first check if the version being used is 1.4 or higher, and only if it is do you use the JSDK 1.4 features.

The class provides only three public static methods, one of which is deprecated. Dozens of useful public static variables handle specific cases. As shown in Listing 2-7, you can get quite a lot of useful information using the SystemUtils class.

Listing 2-7. SystemUtilsTrial

```
package com.commonsbook.chap2;
import org.apache.commons.lang.SystemUtils;

public class SystemUtilsTrial {
    public static void main(String[] args) {
        System.out.println("1) FILE_SEPARATOR =" + SystemUtils.FILE_SEPARATOR);
        System.out.println("2) JAVA_EXT_DIRS =" + SystemUtils.JAVA_EXT_DIRS);
        System.out.println("3) JAVA_HOME =" + SystemUtils.JAVA_HOME);
        System.out.println("4) Is 1.3 + =" +
            SystemUtils.isJavaVersionAtLeast(1.3f));
        System.out.println("5) JAVA_EXT_DIRS =" + SystemUtils.JAVA_EXT_DIRS);
        System.out.println("6) JAVA_VENDOR =" + SystemUtils.JAVA_VENDOR);
        System.out.println("7) OS_NAME =" + SystemUtils.OS_NAME);
    }
}
```

The output upon executing this example on my machine is as follows:

```
1) FILE_SEPARATOR =\
2) JAVA_EXT_DIRS =C:\JDeveloper\jdk\jre\lib\ext
3) JAVA_HOME =C:\JDeveloper\jdk\jre
4) Is 1.3 + =true
5) JAVA_EXT_DIRS =C:\JDeveloper\jdk\jre\lib\ext
6) JAVA_VENDOR =Sun Microsystems Inc.
7) OS_NAME =Windows 2000
```

ClassUtils

The ClassUtils class is a new class introduced with version 2. This class provides static methods that can fetch you more information about a class or an object without having to directly use the Reflection Application Programming Interface (API).

However, think twice before using some of the methods; if your design is proper, you ideally should not have to put such checks in your code. Listing 2-8 shows how to use some of the method provided.

Listing 2-8. ClassUtilsTrial

```
package com.commonsbook.chap2;
import org.apache.commons.lang.ClassUtils;
```

```
public class ClassUtilsTrial {
    public static void main(String[] args) {
        System.out.println("1) Interfaces implemented by java.lang.String >>> " +
            ClassUtils.getAllInterfaces(String.class));
        System.out.println("2) SuperClasses of java.lang.String >>> " +
            ClassUtils.getAllSuperclasses(String.class));
        System.out.println("3) PackageName of a string >>> " +
            ClassUtils.getPackageName("A String", "IfNull"));
        System.out.println("4) Every String is an Object = " +
            ClassUtils.isAssignable(String.class, Object.class));
        System.out.println("5) Every Object is an String = " +
            ClassUtils.isAssignable(Object.class, String.class));
    }
}
```

The output upon executing this code is as follows:

```
1) Interfaces implemented by java.lang.String >>> [interface java.io.Serializable
, interface java.lang.Comparable, interface java.lang.CharSequence]
2) SuperClasses of java.lang.String >>> [class java.lang.Object]
3) PackageName of a string >>> java.lang
4) Every String is an Object = true
5) Every Object is an String = false
```

When using the getPackageName method of ClassUtils, you pass a String object, and because String class lies in the java.lang package, you get that as output. If instead of A String you had passed null, then the string IfNull would have been returned.

StringEscapeUtils

Having to handle Hypertext Markup Language (HTML), JavaScript, Structured Query Language (SQL), and Java simultaneously is very much a part of a Java developer's life. However, generating output in a different format or handling input in a different format can be quite a task.

For example, say you want to display <p>MyName<p> on a Web page. If you just send this as part of the HTML, what would appear on the screen is a new paragraph with the word *MyName* in it. The <p> tags used would not be displayed. What you need to send in the HTML would be this line of code:

```
&lt;p&gt;MyName&lt;p&gt;
```

This would then result in you getting the expected display <p>MyName<p>. The StringEscapeUtils class makes implementing these cases quite simple because it provides ways of converting characters to achieve the expected output. Listing 2-9 shows how you can handle the case just discussed.

Listing 2-9. StringEscapeUtilsTrial

```
package com.commonsbook.chap2;
import org.apache.commons.lang.StringEscapeUtils;

public class StringEscapeUtilsTrial {
    public static void main(String[] args) {
        String strHTMLInput = "<p>MyName<p>";
        String strEscapeHTML = StringEscapeUtils.escapeHtml(strHTMLInput);
        String strUnEscapeHTML = StringEscapeUtils.unescapeHtml(strEscapeHTML);
        System.out.println("Escaped HTML >>> " + strEscapeHTML);
        System.out.println("UnEscaped HTML >>> " + strUnEscapeHTML);
    }
}
```

The output is as follows:

```
Escaped HTML >>> &lt;p&gt;MyName&lt;p&gt;
UnEscaped HTML >>> <p>MyName<p>
```

Apart from escaping HTML, the StringEscapeUtils class also provides methods to achieve similar results with Java, SQL, and JavaScript.

You will now check out the builder package that provides some interesting classes meant to assist in the creation of a few commonly used methods.

Using org.apache.commons.builder

The builder package is an attempt to provide a simple way of generating some of the most commonly used methods in Java classes. The builder package provides builder classes for the equals, toString, hashCode, and compareTo methods.

Providing a proper toString or equals method makes good sense, especially when you are storing data into data objects such as Person, Customer, Player, and so on. Invariably during development the need arises to log all field values and to compare if the contents of two objects are the same.

In Listing 2-10, you will use the various builders to generate an equals, hashCode, and toString method for the class BuilderTrial.

Listing 2-10. BuilderTrial

```java
package com.commonsbook.chap2;
import org.apache.commons.lang.builder.EqualsBuilder;
import org.apache.commons.lang.builder.HashCodeBuilder;
import org.apache.commons.lang.builder.ToStringBuilder;
import org.apache.commons.lang.builder.ToStringStyle;

public class BuilderTrial {
    private String name;
    private int age;

    public BuilderTrial(String name, int age) {
        this.name = name;
        this.age = age;
    }

    public static void main(String[] args) {
        //Create new BuilderTrial instances
        BuilderTrial one = new BuilderTrial("Becker", 35);
        BuilderTrial two = new BuilderTrial("Becker", 35);
        BuilderTrial three = new BuilderTrial("Agassi", 33);

        //one and two hold the same data in different objects
        //three holds different data
        System.out.println("One>>>" + one);
        System.out.println("Two>>>" + two);
        System.out.println("Three>>>" + three);

        System.out.println("one equals two? " + one.equals(two));
        System.out.println("one equals three? " + one.equals(three));

        //As one and two hold the same data, the same hashcode is returned.
        System.out.println("One HashCode>>> " + one.hashCode());
        System.out.println("Two HashCode>>> " + two.hashCode());
        System.out.println("Three HashCode>>> " + three.hashCode());
    }

    public boolean equals(Object objCompared) {
        if (!(objCompared instanceof BuilderTrial)) {
            return false;
        }

        BuilderTrial rhs = (BuilderTrial) objCompared;
```

```
            return new EqualsBuilder().append(name, rhs.name).append(age, rhs.age)
                                .isEquals();
    }

    public String toString() {
        return new ToStringBuilder(this,
            ToStringStyle.MULTI_LINE_STYLE).append("Name",
            name).append("Age", age).toString();
    }

    public int hashCode() {
        return new HashCodeBuilder(15, 19).append(name).append(age).toHashCode();
    }
}
```

The output upon running this example is as follows:

```
One>>>com.commonsbook.chap2.BuilderTrial@5[
  Name=Becker
  Age=35
]
Two>>>com.commonsbook.chap2.BuilderTrial@6[
  Name=Becker
  Age=35
]
Three>>>com.commonsbook.chap2.BuilderTrial@7[
  Name=Agassi
  Age=33
]
one equals two? true
one equals three? false
One HashCode>>> -923455822
Two HashCode>>> -923455822
Three HashCode>>> -1433293806
```

EqualsBuilder

The equals method is meant to check if the contents of one object are equal to that of another. The objects might be distinct, but their contents should be equal. To compare two objects with, say, five fields each, you can either write the code to check each variable and return true if all values match, or use EqualsBuilder. Apart from having to put in the effort of writing this code, a common problem is the occurrence of null values that cause NullPointerException to be thrown.

A better and more elegant approach is to use EqualsBuilder. You need only to create an instance of EqualsBuilder and then call the append methods provided for each of the fields you want to compare.

The EqualsBuilder class provides 18 append methods that are capable of comparing primitives, objects, and even arrays. Each append method returns a modified EqualsBuilder object on which you finally call the isEquals method to get the boolean true/false you expect. Any new field additions mean only the addition of an append call in the equals method.

In the example, to check if two objects are equal, you compare the values of the fields name and age. Because instance one and instance two both hold the same data, the values match and equals method returns true. Object three has field values that do not match with the values of fields in one and resultantly equals returns false.

ToStringBuilder

The toString method is a method that is ubiquitous to all Java code. In some cases, you might call it explicitly, and in other cases the toString method might get called automatically. However, in either case, the output generated by the toString method is critical to getting proper text displayed or messages logged.

The toString method, being part of java.lang.Object, ensures that every Java object created has a toString method. The ToStringBuilder class is a handy solution to ensure that the toString method for a class generates a sensible and well-formatted message. The ideal toString method should display details of the object and the contents of the fields within the object.

Similarly to EqualsBuilder, for the ToStringBuilder you need to create a new instance of ToStringBuilder, specify the style of display, and then keep appending all the details you want to be generated in the string returned by the toString method. Once you are done appending these details, you call the toString method provided by the ToStringBuilder class to get the actual string that the method will return.

In this example, the BuilderTrial object has two fields, and you want the toString method to display the field name and values for both of these fields. The ToStringBuilder class provides many append methods, and you have the option to just state the name of the field or also provide a description for it. In this example, you state the field names' description string as Name and Age; however, you could very well have named them Albert and Einstein.

The ToStringBuilder constructor accepts the name of the style to be used for the string generation. This example has used MULTI_LINE_STYLE, which has led to the fields being displayed on separate lines in the output. The style parameter is optional, and if not specified, the default style as defined by the field DEFAULT_STYLE in the class ToStringStyle is used. You can also set the default style using the setDefaultStyle method in the class ToStringBuilder.

The ToStringStyle class provides four private static classes that you can use to change the output format. These classes provide for a default style, a multiline style, a no field names style, and a simple style. In most cases, using one of these should do the job. However, if you want to customize the display further, you can use the class StandardToStringStyle that extends ToStringStyle or write a new class extending either ToStringStyle or StandardToStringStyle.

HashCodeBuilder

Hashcodes for objects are meant to be unique and representative of the contents of an object. However, writing custom logic that does this for you is not an easy task. The HashCodeBuilder class is a way to quickly have hashcode logic in place that generates a sound hashcode based on the current contents of an object.

In the example, you create a new instance of the HashCodeBuilder class using two randomly chosen odd and nonzero numbers. Prime numbers and different numbers for different classes are recommended.

 CAUTION *Passing an even number or zero will cause a* java.lang.IllegalArgumentException *to be thrown.*

Once you create the HashCodeBuilder instance, you use the append method to append the fields you want the hashcode to be representative of. Once these appends are done, you call the toHashCode method to generate and return the hashcode generated.

 NOTE *In the example, for objects one and two, although they are distinct objects because their field values are the same, the hash-code generated is the same. By definition, when two objects are equal, their hashcodes must be the same.*

Using Reflection

Instead of the methods used earlier, would it not be an easier option if you did not have to specify the field names and your methods looked as follows?

```
public boolean equals(Object obj) {
    return EqualsBuilder.reflectionEquals(this, obj);
}
```

```
public String toString() {
    return ToStringBuilder.reflectionToString(this
            , ToStringStyle.MULTI_LINE_STYLE);
}

public int hashCode() {
    return HashCodeBuilder.reflectionHashCode(this);
}
```

This is an option you have because all the builders provide this feature where the builder uses reflection to determine the field name and values for the object in question. This method, however, is slower and gives you far less control over the actual creation of the hashcode or the string generated by toString. This methodology will work even if the fields are private.

Using org.apache.commons.exception

The exception package provides the functionality to nest exceptions within other exceptions. Nesting exceptions is commonly used on projects. However, until JSDK 1.4 and this section in the Lang component emerged, you had to manually code this nesting mechanism.

The nesting capability of Lang not only enables you to store exceptions within other exceptions but also track the exact flow of exceptions. You can trace the root cause of an exception and the exact path it followed until the exception was finally caught and handled. Listing 2-11 shows an example where you nest an exception within a custom exception that you create.

Listing 2-11. ExceptionTrial

```
package com.commonsbook.chap2;
import org.apache.commons.lang.exception.ExceptionUtils;
import org.apache.commons.lang.exception.NestableException;

public class ExceptionTrial {
    public static void main(String[] args) {
        try {
            middleMeth();
        } catch (Exception e) {
            System.out.println(
                "Number of Throwable objects in the exception chain is: " +
                ExceptionUtils.getThrowableCount(e));
            e.printStackTrace();
        }
    }
```

```java
    public static void middleMeth() throws Exception {
        try {
            theRoot();
        } catch (Exception e) {
            throw new ApplicationException("Packaged into Nestable", e);
        }
    }

    public static void theRoot() throws Exception {
        throw new Exception("The Root Exception");
    }
}


/**
 * An application specific exception
 */
class ApplicationException extends NestableException {
    public ApplicationException(String msg, Throwable cause) {
        super(msg, cause);
    }
}
```

In this example, the exception is thrown from the method theRoot. Here the exception thrown is of type Exception. However, in the method middleMeth, the exception is caught and nested into a custom exception named ApplicationException. Finally, the main method that calls the method middleMeth handles the exception and prints the stack trace. The output generated is as follows:

```
com.commonsbook.chap2.ApplicationException: Packaged into Nestable
  at com.commonsbook.chap2.ExceptionTrial.middleMeth(ExceptionTrial.java:21)
  at com.commonsbook.chap2.ExceptionTrial.main(ExceptionTrial.java:8)
Caused by: java.lang.Exception: The Root Exception
  at com.commonsbook.chap2.ExceptionTrial.theRoot(ExceptionTrial.java:26)
  at com.commonsbook.chap2.ExceptionTrial.middleMeth(ExceptionTrial.java:19)
  ... 1 more
Number of Throwable objects in the exception chain is: 2
```

The output depicts that the root exception occurred in the method theRoot and then was rethrown in the method middleMeth as an ApplicationException. This information can be particularly useful while debugging applications.

JSDK 1.4 has introduced the capability to nest exceptions within other exceptions, so you can do something similar using JSDK 1.4. However, if your application might have to run on earlier versions, using NestableException provided by the Lang component is a better option than having to write new code for the nesting. The Lang classes are capable of handling JSDK 1.4 exceptions as well as those thrown by earlier versions.

To achieve nesting of exceptions using JSDK 1.4, you need to utilize two new constructors of the java.lang.Throwable class that have been introduced with version 1.4. These constructors can accept another exception as the cause for an exception. So a chain of exceptions gets maintained, and no exceptions are lost.

ExceptionUtils class is a utility class that provides many static methods to examine exceptions and extract more information out of it. The example used one of these methods to get the number of Throwable objects in the exception chain.

Using org.apache.commons.enum

The enum package provides type-safe enums. An *enum* stands for an enumeration or a list. So you can have an enum of colors, states, countries, components, and so on. The enum implementation is type safe because it will only accept objects of one type. So you cannot have an enum where some elements are of type X and some of type Y. Those with a C language background should be familiar with enums; however, the Java language does not have any enum support built into the JSDK. The enum package is meant to provide this missing enum capability for the Java world. It provides an abstract class named Enum. Enum being abstract, you need to extend Enum to create your own enums. You can provide the methods required directly in every class you create; the alternative is to use the EnumUtils class. Listing 2-12 creates an enum of some of the Commons components and then uses the EnumUtils class to access the enum created.

Listing 2-12. EnumTrial

```
package com.commonsbook.chap2;
import org.apache.commons.lang.enum.Enum;
import org.apache.commons.lang.enum.EnumUtils;

import java.util.Iterator;
import java.util.Map;

public class EnumTrial {
    public static void main(String[] args) {
        Enum e1 = EnumUtils.getEnum(ComponentsEnum.class, "Validator");
        System.out.println("Name of Enum >>>" + e1.getName());

        Iterator itr1 = EnumUtils.iterator(ComponentsEnum.class);
```

```
        while (itr1.hasNext()) {
            System.out.println(itr1.next());
        }

        Map map1 = EnumUtils.getEnumMap(ComponentsEnum.class);
        System.out.println("Map Size >>>" + map1.size());
        System.out.println("Get Logging from Enum >>>" + map1.get("Logging"));
    }
}



/**
 * An enumeration of some Commons components
 */
class ComponentsEnum extends Enum {
    public static final ComponentsEnum LANG = new ComponentsEnum("Lang");
    public static final ComponentsEnum LOGGING = new ComponentsEnum("Logging");
    public static final ComponentsEnum COLLECTIONS = new ComponentsEnum(
            "Collections");
    public static final ComponentsEnum VALIDATOR = new ComponentsEnum(
            "Validator");
    public static final ComponentsEnum DIGESTER = new ComponentsEnum("Digester");

    public ComponentsEnum(String componentName) {
        super(componentName);
    }
}
```

In this example, the ComponentsEnum class extends Enum and creates a static final instance of ComponentsEnum for all those components you want to be part of the enum. Next, you provide a constructor that just passes the component name to the constructor of the superclass.

In the EnumTrial class, you use the methods provided by the EnumUtils class to access specific elements in the enum, to get an iterator for all elements in the enum, and to get a Map holding key/value pairs for all elements in the enum.

 TIP *Because enums are not part of the basic Java API yet, I do not recommend their usage. Someone else trying to understand your code might not be able to comprehend the usage. Enums are expected to make an appearance in the next JSDK release, however.*

The output upon executing the code is as follows:

```
Name of Enum >>>Validator
ComponentsEnum[Lang]
ComponentsEnum[Logging]
ComponentsEnum[Collections]
ComponentsEnum[Validator]
ComponentsEnum[Digester]
Map Size >>>5
Get Logging from Enum >>>ComponentsEnum[Logging]
```

You will now look at the math package, which provides some basic math utilities.

Using `org.apache.commons.math`

The math package is a new package introduced in version 2. As yet, the functionality provided is primarily related to easily converting between data types and working with a range of values. This package is not expected to go very far because a separate Math component also exists as part of Jakarta Commons and is the one meant to handle advanced math requirements.

The math package provides range classes that can be used to create a range of primitives: double, float, int, and long. You can easily create a range by passing the minimum value and maximum value for the range. You can then use this range to check if a value lies within a certain range.

The two classes in the package that provide many utility functions are NumberUtils and RandomUtils. Listing 2-13 shows how to use the features of these classes.

Listing 2-13. MathUtilsTrial

```
package com.commonsbook.chap2;
import org.apache.commons.lang.math.NumberUtils;
import org.apache.commons.lang.math.RandomUtils;

import java.math.BigDecimal;

public class MathUtilsTrial {
    public static void main(String[] args) {
        //Compare two double values
        System.out.println("(FIRST > SECOND) >>> " +
            NumberUtils.compare(2.11, 1.11));
```

```
    System.out.println("(FIRST < SECOND) >>> " +
        NumberUtils.compare(1.11, 2.11));
    System.out.println("(FIRST == SECOND) >>> " +
        NumberUtils.compare(1.11, 1.11));

    //Create a BigDecimal from a String
    BigDecimal bDecimal = NumberUtils.createBigDecimal("123456789");

    //Check if a String contains only digits
    System.out.println("Is Digits >>> " + NumberUtils.isDigits("123.123"));

    //Check if a String is a valid number
    System.out.println("Is Number >>> " + NumberUtils.isNumber("123.123"));

    //Get MAX value from an array
    System.out.println("MAX >>> " +
        NumberUtils.max(new double[] { 3.33, 8.88, 1.11 }));

    //Convert String to int. If value invalid, return default value.
    System.out.println("String to Int >>> " +
        NumberUtils.stringToInt("ABCD", 77));

    //Random Value Generation
    System.out.println("Random double >>> " + RandomUtils.nextDouble());
    System.out.println("Random float >>> " + RandomUtils.nextFloat());
    System.out.println("Random int >>> " + RandomUtils.nextInt());
    }
}
```

The compare method returns the following:

- 0 if two values are equal

- 1 if the first value is greater than the second

- -1 if the first value is less than the second

NumberUtils also provides other create methods that return the wrapper classes Integer, Double, and Float, as well as Long, Number, and BigInteger. The createNumber method is particularly interesting. Whatever value you might pass it, it is able to figure out what type it is and create an instance of the appropriate java.lang.Number subclass. The NumberUtils class is particularly good at finding the maximum and minimum values from arrays of various data types and also from a set of three numbers.

The output for this example is as follows:

```
(FIRST > SECOND) >>> 1
(FIRST < SECOND) >>> -1
(FIRST == SECOND) >>> 0
Is Digits >>> false
Is Number >>> true
MAX >>> 8.88
String to Int >>> 77
Random double >>> 0.2720979622981403
Random float >>> 0.8221457
Random int >>> 738187848
```

Using `org.apache.commons.time`

The time package is a nice addition to version 2. It provides many features
to quickly fetch dates and format those into predefined as well as user-defined
formats.

Although there are many classes listed in the package, you do not need to
look beyond three or four key classes. Although there is a lot of functionality
to generate string output from Date and Calendar, there is not much that does
things the other way around. For that, you still have to use the existing Java
options.

Listing 2-14 shows how to use the date formatting and other capabilities of
the package.

Listing 2-14. TimeTrial

```java
package com.commonsbook.chap2;
import org.apache.commons.lang.time.DateFormatUtils;
import org.apache.commons.lang.time.DateUtils;
import org.apache.commons.lang.time.StopWatch;

import java.util.Calendar;
import java.util.Date;
import java.util.Iterator;

public class TimeTrial {
    public static void main(String[] args) {
        //Format Date into dd-MM-yyyy
        System.out.println("1) dd-MM-yyyy >>>" +
            DateFormatUtils.format(new Date(), "dd-MM-yyyy"));
```

```
//Format Date into SMTP_DATETIME_FORMAT
System.out.println("2) SMTP_DATETIME_FORMAT >>>" +
    DateFormatUtils.SMTP_DATETIME_FORMAT.format(new Date()));

//Format Date into ISO_DATE_FORMAT
System.out.println("3) ISO_DATE_FORMAT >>>" +
    DateFormatUtils.ISO_DATE_FORMAT.format(new Date()));

//Format milliseconds in long
System.out.println("4) MMM dd yy HH:mm >>>" +
    DateFormatUtils.format(System.currentTimeMillis(), "MMM dd yy HH:mm"));

//Format milliseconds in long using UTC time zone
System.out.println("5) MM/dd/yy HH:mm >>>" +
    DateFormatUtils.formatUTC(System.currentTimeMillis(),
        "MM/dd/yy HH:mm"));

StopWatch stWatch = new StopWatch();

//Start StopWatch
stWatch.start();

//Get iterator for all days in a week starting Monday
Iterator itr = DateUtils.iterator(new Date(),
        DateUtils.RANGE_WEEK_MONDAY);

while (itr.hasNext()) {
    Calendar gCal = (Calendar) itr.next();
    System.out.println(gCal.getTime());
}

//Stop StopWatch
stWatch.stop();
System.out.println("Time Taken >>" + stWatch.getTime());
    }
}
```

In this example, you use SMTP_DATETIME_FORMAT and ISO_DATE_FORMAT to format the current date. Seven other formats are defined as static fields in the DateFormatUtils class. If you need to use formats beyond these, you of course have the option of defining your own format.

The output of the code running on my machine is as follows:

```
1) dd-MM-yyyy >>>09-12-2003
2) SMTP_DATETIME_FORMAT >>>Tue, 09 Dec 2003 00:34:47 +0530
3) ISO_DATE_FORMAT >>>2003-12-09
4) MMM dd yy HH:mm >>>Dec 09 03 00:34
5) MM/dd/yy HH:mm >>>12/08/03 19:04
Mon Dec 08 00:00:00 GMT+05:30 2003
Tue Dec 09 00:00:00 GMT+05:30 2003
Wed Dec 10 00:00:00 GMT+05:30 2003
Thu Dec 11 00:00:00 GMT+05:30 2003
Fri Dec 12 00:00:00 GMT+05:30 2003
Sat Dec 13 00:00:00 GMT+05:30 2003
Sun Dec 14 00:00:00 GMT+05:30 2003
Time Taken >>31
```

 NOTE *The formats are case sensitive. So although* MM *stands for day of the month,* mm *stands for minutes. This is the same convention used by standard Java classes.*

The functionality to get an iterator for the current week or month is a truly interesting one. This can come in handy while creating and displaying calendars or schedules. The StopWatch can also come in handy if you are trying to time your methods in a performance optimization exercise.

Summary

In this chapter, you learned about the Lang component and most of the important classes that are part of the component. The Lang component is surely one of the simplest to pick up and adopt. It is highly unlikely that the Lang component has nothing to offer you right away.

If you are not sure about adopting Commons components, I suggest you start with the Lang component. Convey to everyone in your team that all new utility code will be accepted only if it is proven that the Lang component does not provide the required functionality.

Of course, there will be unique cases where custom code is required, but once the entire team has had a look at the Lang methods, adoption should be relatively smooth and without resistance.

CHAPTER 3

Using the Logging Component

WHAT IS THE ONE THING that has to be used across all types of applications? Yes, of course: some kind of logging mechanism. You might refer to it as *logging* or some other name, but you cannot develop any real application without having to log some information either to check and debug some functionality or to track unexpected errors.

In this chapter, you will look at the Logging component that has become quite popular lately. Even applications such as the Tomcat server and the Struts framework are using it to handle their logging requirements. Table 3-1 shows the component details.

Table 3-1. Component Details

Name	Version	Package
Logging	1.0.3	org.apache.commons.logging

Understanding Logging APIs

Before the emergence of the logging Application Programming Interfaces (APIs) of today, the only real logging mechanisms used in Java applications were System.out and System.err. You could use these to log debug and error messages. However, considering the growing complexity of applications—especially with the emergence of Java 2 Enterprise Edition (J2EE)—it became imperative for applications to log all information that would assist in debugging a program and all details of any errors and exceptions that might occur. The crude mechanism of using System.out and System.err was not good enough to fulfill this need.

What was required was a consistent logging mechanism that was easy to use, that could log information to various devices in a properly structured format, and that made errors easily traceable. The three alternatives that fulfill these criteria, and that need to be considered before you decide on a logging mechanism, are Log4j, Avalon LogKit, and Java Development Kit (JDK) 1.4 logging.

Log4j

Log4j is the solution that provides developers with a powerful API to maintain proper logs. You can find Log4j at http://jakarta.apache.org/log4j, and apart from the documentation on the site, other Web sources as well as books talk about Log4j in detail. Although the JDK 1.4 logging API is similar to Log4j, the Commons Logging component also revolves around the idea of logging as understood in the Log4j world.

The big advantage that Log4j presents over the earlier modes of logging is that you can easily configure it at runtime, and you can even leave logging statements in your source code with negligible effect on the application's performance. Log4j also has the concept of logging levels. Based on where in the development lifecycle a project is, you can easily configure Log4j so that only certain types of messages are logged while the rest are ignored. Having bare minimal statements logged is important because Java Input/Output (I/O) takes quite some time and affects performance.

Another advantage of using Log4j is that it has been around for some time now and is a well-tested solution. Log4j is JDK 1.1.*x* compatible, and being part of the Apache family should ensure that development of Log4j continues. Using Log4j can get quite complex if you intend to use all of its features; however, for most applications, the basic and easy-to-use functionality is good enough.

With Log4j, you do not just log a message. You have to log it at a certain level. The five levels supported by Log4j are debug, info, warn, error, and fatal. Of these, debug logs the least critical messages, and fatal messages generally log major failures and exceptions that might crash the entire application. Usually, you want to configure Log4j so that during development all levels of messages are logged, and once the application goes into production, only warn, error, and fatal messages are logged.

Avalon LogKit

You can find Avalon LogKit at http://avalon.apache.org/logkit; it is another logging alternative you can consider. It provides features such as pattern-based formatting of output and filtering of output. The logging levels for LogKit are debug, info, warn, error, and fatal_error.

Being part of the Avalon framework means that LogKit enjoys a good user community, but compared to the alternatives, LogKit is not that popular of a tool. Also, I found the documentation and examples from the site and from other sources to be a little short of satisfactory.

JDK1.4 Logging

An important addition to JDK 1.4 is its support for logging. Log4j used to be the only real player in the logging API space, but JDK 1.4 has changed that. A lot of new development today is using the JDK 1.4 logging API to handle logging needs. The big question before developers is this: Why use a third-party API if you are developing an application based on JDK 1.4 and have a logging API already at hand? Now that logging has become part of JDK 1.4, it is bound to continue and improve in future versions of the JDK.

The JDK logging API is part of the package java.util.logging and has similar features and usage to Log4j. The logging API has functionality such as writing a log to various devices, buffering the log in memory, formatting the log, and even generating the log in an Extensible Markup Language (XML) layout. Although a log in XML layout is not as easily readable as an ordinary log, the advantage of having the log as XML is that the log can be easily parsed using XML parsers or can be transformed using Extensible Stylesheet Language (XSL).

The logging levels as provided by the JDK logging are as follows:

- **Severe**: This level of logging is used in cases where the system is likely to crash and requires some immediate fix to be provided.

- **Warning**: This level of logging is used for errors that are serious but that do not really require the engineer to rush to the office in the middle of the night to provide a fix.

- **Info**: This level is meant to provide more information, which is nothing special.

- **Config**: This level is to log configuration messages.

- **Fine, finer, and finest**: These levels of logging provide detailed information.

Although this chapter is about the Commons Logging component, I have not listed it as one of the alternatives because rating it on par with Log4j or the JDK 1.4 logging API would be unfair. The Commons Logging component is not a separate logging mechanism but is more of a wrapper over the existing ones.

Using the Logging Component

All three alternatives discussed earlier provide a sound logging mechanism for Java. So it does not make sense for the Commons project to also provide a logging alternative that works along the same lines as the existing ones.

Therefore, the Logging component is not an alternative to Log4j or the JDK 1.4 logging API. The Commons component is an API that sits on top of the other APIs to provide you with a common logging API to use in the source code. Figure 3-1 shows that the application code interacts only with the Commons Logging component's `Log` interface, and the Logging component, based on its configuration, decides which mode of logging to actually use.

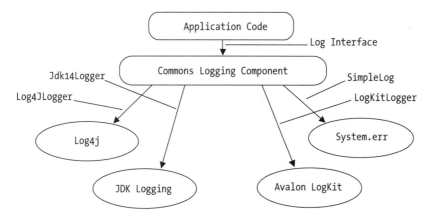

Figure 3-1. The Commons logging architecture

Figure 3-1 also points out the actual `Logger` class that is used in each case. The loggers are the actual implementations that have code specific to a particular logging mechanism.

Logging Levels

The logging levels for the Logging component are similar to the levels for Log4j. The only additional level is the `trace` level. The other levels, their names, and significance are the same as with Log4j:

- **Fatal**: Critical errors out of which the system is unlikely to recover

- **Error**: Critical errors, but the system will survive

- **Warn**: Errors that cause no immediate damage but that need to be pointed out

- **Info**: General information such as system stopped, started, and so on

- **Debug**: Detailed debugging information, meant to assist developers during development or with bug fixing

- **Trace**: An additional level that logs detailed information and is not present in Log4j

Usage

Using any of the logging APIs in your Java code is really quite simple. The slightly difficult part lies in understanding how they work and being able to configure your logging mechanism to get the desired result.

Before learning about the technicalities of the Logging component, you will look at a simple Java application that has a main method and uses the Log interface methods (see Listing 3-1). You will then move step by step through this application and try to understand how the Logging component works.

Listing 3-1. LoggingTrial *Class*

```
package com.commonsbook.chap3;
import org.apache.commons.logging.Log;
import org.apache.commons.logging.LogFactory;

public class LoggingTrial {
    public static void main(String[] args) {
        //Get new Log instance for this class
        Log log = LogFactory.getLog(LoggingTrial.class);

        //Which Logger is being Used?
        System.out.println("The Log being used >>> " + log);

        //Create a dummy exception to depict exception logging
        Exception e = new Exception("A DUMMY EXCEPTION");

        //Log TRACE if enabled
        if (log.isTraceEnabled()) {
            log.trace("TRACE TEST");
            log.trace("TRACE TEST", e);
        }
```

```
    //Log DEBUG if enabled
    if (log.isDebugEnabled()) {
        log.debug("DEBUG TEST");
        log.debug("DEBUG TEST", e);
    }

    //Log INFO if enabled
    if (log.isInfoEnabled()) {
        log.info("INFO TEST");
        log.info("INFO TEST", e);
    }

    //Log WARN if enabled
    if (log.isWarnEnabled()) {
        log.warn("WARN TEST");
        log.warn("WARN TEST", e);
    }

    //Log ERROR if enabled
    if (log.isErrorEnabled()) {
        log.error("ERROR TEST");
        log.error("ERROR TEST", e);
    }

    //Log FATAL if enabled
    if (log.isFatalEnabled()) {
        log.fatal("FATAL TEST");
        log.fatal("FATAL TEST", e);
    }
  }
}
```

This code is really all there is to the coding aspect of using the Logging component. You do not even need to look at any other code examples because this is how simple it is to use the Logging component. You do not have to consider any other logging method beyond the methods provided in the org.apache.commons.logging.Log interface. This example covers all the methods provided. The dummy exception had to be used to invoke the methods where a Throwable object is also passed as a parameter to be able to log the details of the exception caused. You do not use any of the API-specific classes of Log4j or the JDK 1.4 logging API. The classes used are all strictly part of the Logging component.

Listing 3-2 shows the output upon executing this class—without any special configuration, where the Log4j library is not in the CLASSPATH, and without using JDK 1.4.

Listing 3-2. LoggingTrial *Output*

```
The Log being used >>> org.apache.commons.logging.impl.SimpleLog@2
[INFO] LoggingTrial - -INFO TEST
[INFO] LoggingTrial - -INFO TEST <java.lang.Exception: A DUMMY
 EXCEPTION>java.lang.Exception: A DUMMY EXCEPTION
        void com.commonsbook.chap3.LoggingTrial.main(java.lang.String[])
                LoggingTrial.java:16

[WARN] LoggingTrial - -WARN TEST
[WARN] LoggingTrial - -WARN TEST <java.lang.Exception: A DUMMY
 EXCEPTION>java.lang.Exception: A DUMMY EXCEPTION
        void com.commonsbook.chap3.LoggingTrial.main(java.lang.String[])
                LoggingTrial.java:16

[ERROR] LoggingTrial - -ERROR TEST
[ERROR] LoggingTrial - -ERROR TEST <java.lang.Exception: A DUMMY
 EXCEPTION>java.lang.Exception: A DUMMY EXCEPTION
        void com.commonsbook.chap3.LoggingTrial.main(java.lang.String[])
                LoggingTrial.java:16

[FATAL] LoggingTrial - -FATAL TEST
[FATAL] LoggingTrial - -FATAL TEST <java.lang.Exception: A DUMMY
 EXCEPTION>java.lang.Exception: A DUMMY EXCEPTION
        void com.commonsbook.chap3.LoggingTrial.main(java.lang.String[])
                LoggingTrial.java:16
```

Now I will explain how this application works. The first requirement is to get a Log instance. For that, you use the static getLog method of the LogFactory class. You specify the class name so that a Log instance for that particular class is created. If an instance for that class is already present, that instance can be reused.

The LogFactory class plays an important role because nowhere in the code do you specify which logging API you intend to use. So it is up to the LogFactory class to decide which API to use based on a few rules. Once that is deduced, an instance of the corresponding Log has to be created and returned.

You have the option of using a different factory than the default LogFactoryImpl by specifying the system property named org.apache.commons.logging.LogFactory or by specifying that property in a property file. If these properties are not found, LogFactoryImpl is used, which should serve the purpose very well.

LogFactoryImpl decides which logging implementation to use by following these rules in this order:

1. Check for a configuration attribute named `org.apache.commons.logging.Log`. The implementation class should be the value of the attribute.

2. Check the system property named `org.apache.commons.logging.Log`.

3. Log4j is the default logging mechanism for the Logging component. So if the Log4j classes are found, use `Log4JLogger`.

4. If JDK 1.4 classes are found, use the JDK 1.4 logging mechanism and create an instance of `Jdk14Logger`.

5. If all the previous rules fail to provide an answer as to which logger to use, use the `SimpleLog` implementation that is part of the component and log all messages to `System.err`.

In Listing 3-1, `SimpleLog` gets used because you did not specify the required properties or have Log4j or JDK 1.4 accessible. The first line of Listing 3-2 tells you which `Logger` was used.

 NOTE *If the default logging level is not specified,* `SimpleLog` *uses* `info` *as the minimum level and only logs messages of levels higher than* `info`*. As a result, debug and trace messages are not logged.*

To switch over to JDK1.4, you can either specify `org.apache.commons.logging.impl.Jdk14Logger` as the `org.apache.commons.logging.Log` property value or just ensure that the first three rules fail and that you are using JDK 1.4 or higher.

To switch to Log4j, you can specify the `org.apache.commons.logging.Log` property value as `org.apache.commons.logging.impl.Log4JLogger` or make the Log4j library and classes available in the `CLASSPATH` or in the `WEB-INF/lib` directory in the case of Web applications, and as per the third rule, Log4j will be used.

 CAUTION *With Log4j, you also need to provide a* `log4j.properties` *file that specifies the appenders to be used. If this file is not found in the* `CLASSPATH`*, you will get a "No appenders could be found for logger" error message.*

Configuration

Configuring the Logging component requires some skill, but using it is simple. Configuration errors can give you some irritating errors to tackle. To configure the Logging component, you need to be familiar with some property files.

In most cases, you can choose between directly setting a system property or setting that property in a property file. Using a property file is certainly a better alternative, and the only task you then need to do is to make that property file available in the CLASSPATH. In most cases, you can change the name of the property file referenced by setting a system property so your property files can have names other than common-logging.properties, log4j.properties, and so on.

 NOTE *Although the Logging component interacts with other logging APIs, it takes no responsibility for configuring those APIs. So, the rules for configuring Log4j stay the same even if you are using the Commons Logging component.*

---

commons-logging.properties

The commons-logging.properties file is the property file where you can specify properties solely related to how the Commons Logging component works. To change the logging implementation being used, you can use *any one* of these property definitions:

```
org.apache.commons.logging.Log=org.apache.commons.logging.impl.Log4JLogger
org.apache.commons.logging.Log=org.apache.commons.logging.impl.SimpleLog
org.apache.commons.logging.Log=org.apache.commons.logging.impl.LogKitLogger
org.apache.commons.logging.Log=org.apache.commons.logging.impl.NoOpLog
org.apache.commons.logging.Log=org.apache.commons.logging.impl.Jdk14Logger
```

Based on this property value and the five steps listed earlier, the actual logging implementation to be used will be decided.

simplelog.properties

If none of the other logging implementations can be used, the Logging component provides a SimpleLog capability that logs the output to System.err. Even this logging can be configured using the simplelog.properties file.

You can specify the following properties:

- **org.apache.commons.logging.simplelog.defaultlog**: The value for this property defines which level of logging should be used by default. If this property is not found, only messages higher than level info are logged.

- **org.apache.commons.logging.simplelog.log.xxxxx**: The logging level for a specific instance of SimpleLog.

- **org.apache.commons.logging.simplelog.showlogname**: This shows the log name; the default value is `false`.

- **org.apache.commons.logging.simplelog.showShortLogname**: This shows a short log name; the default value is `true`.

- **org.apache.commons.logging.simplelog.showdatetime**: This logs the date and time for every log. The default value is `false`.

log4j.properties

To use Log4j as your logging mechanism, you need to create the `log4j.properties` file. Although discussing Log4j configuration is beyond the scope of this book, the following is an example `log4j.properties` file that logs all output to a file named `testLog4JLogging.log`:

```
log4j.rootLogger=, AFile
log4j.appender.AFile=org.apache.log4j.FileAppender

//Filename is testLog4JLogging.log
log4j.appender.AFile.File=testLog4JLogging.log

//Do not append to existing file. Earlier contents lost
log4j.appender.AFile.Append=false

# Use PatternLayout.
log4j.appender.AFile.layout=org.apache.log4j.PatternLayout
log4j.appender.AFile.layout.ConversionPattern=%p %t %c - %m %n
```

For a detailed discussion on Log4j configuration, point your browser to `http://jakarta.apache.org/log4j`.

Web Applications

Because most Java development these days is in the world of J2EE and Web applications, you will now quickly look at logging in Web applications.

A Web application has a definite structure, where the `WEB-INF` directory and its subdirectories all play specific roles. To use the Commons Logging component, you need the following files:

Libraries: The libraries—the Java Archive (JAR) files—hold the classes for the Logging component, Log4j, LogKit, and so on. So to use any of these, it is imperative that the corresponding classes be found. The WEB-INF/lib directory is the place to put the libraries being used. Although placing the libraries in the common lib directory for the server being used would also get the job done, that would not be the proper way to go about it. It is best to maintain application-specific libraries as part of the application.

Properties: The property files are key to configuring your logging mechanism. The easiest way to ensure that the *.properties files for a particular Web application are found and do not interfere with property files for other applications is to dump the property files into the WEB-INF/classes directory. The server will be able to find the property files placed here.

Summary

The Logging component is a useful little tool that has grown quite popular. Switching between logging mechanisms is easily possible using the Logging component, and using it is also very simple.

However, you need to answer some questions before choosing the Logging component:

- Do I need any API-specific features that would be lost if I use Commons logging because the Logging component provides the set of features that are only common across multiple APIs?

- How likely is it that I would want to change my logging mechanism sometime in the future?

- Am I looking for compatibility with versions prior to JDK 1.4? If not, directly using JDK 1.4 logging could be a solution.

- Why would I ever want to leave Log4j, after it has worked so well for so long and it certainly enjoys great community support?

Once you have answered these questions, deciding whether the Commons Logging component is the right choice should not be very difficult.

CHAPTER 4

Using the Validator Component

VALIDATING USER INPUT is one of the most bug-prone tasks in a project. If you have to use JavaScript for client-side validations, your task becomes even more difficult because if some script works well on browser X, it is likely that it will not do the expected task on browser Y. Also, considering that the same validation logic keeps repeating across pages and even projects, validation code is a great candidate for reuse.

In this chapter, you will learn about the Validator component that is meant to make validations simple and easily configurable. Like some other Commons components, the Validator component also has its origins in the Struts framework. The chapter first covers how to use the Validator component without Struts and later shows how to use it in tandem with Struts. Table 4-1 shows the component details.

Table 4-1. Component Details

Name	Version	Package
Validator	1.0.2	org.apache.commons.validator

Introducing the Validator Component

The Validator component is a framework you can use to take the drudgery out of writing validation code. The Validator component comes with a built-in validation capability for some common validations. The Validator component began as part of the Struts framework; however, now the validator code that is specific to Struts has been moved into a Struts validator, and the common validation capability is part of the Commons Validator component.

The advantages of using the validator framework are as follows:

- Validation rules can be defined in separate Extensible Markup Language (XML) files.

- Validation rules can be changed without having to touch the source code.

- Built-in validations handle most of the common scenarios.

- Minimal coding is required.

- It is a proven solution used by many applications, especially Struts applications.

The validator's integration with Struts version 1.1 means that it is now even easier to use the validator with Struts. However, there is nothing that restricts validator usage to just Web applications. For any application that involves extensive user input and validation, the validator is a good framework to choose.

Just downloading the latest version of validator from http://jakarta.apache.org/ does not suffice, however, because the validator depends on some other Commons components. The validator version I use in this chapter is version 1.0.2. The validator's external dependencies are as follows:

- Commons BeanUtils: Version 1.0 or later.

- Commons Collections: Version 1.0 or later.

- Commons Digester: Version 1.0 or later.

- Commons Logging: Version 1.0 or later.

- Digester requires an XML parser such as Xerces that can be downloaded from http://xml.apache.org/.

Unlike many of the other Commons components, the validator documentation—at least as of this writing—is just not up to par. There is little explanation to be found on the site or as part of the Application Programming Interface (API) documentation. This is a little disappointing because unless you are forced to use it or have to write about it, you probably would not spend much time trying to learn such tools. The documentation of the Struts validator is good, and the many books and other Web site resources available augment the basic documentation. However, if you want to use the validator for non-Struts applications, the documentation is lacking.

To understand the validator as a component independent of Struts, the source code for the Validator component and the JUnit-based test cases can help. JUnit is a simple testing framework that you can find at http://junit.org/.

You will first look at how you can use the validator independent of Struts and later look at the validator's integration with Struts.

Using the Validator Independently

While using the validator with Struts, you have the luxury of lots of reference material as well as some ready-made validations. However, things do get a little tougher if you intend to use the validator independent of Struts. The API specifications are not the greatest, and other reference material is conspicuous by its absence.

So to use the validator independent of Struts, I suggest you first develop a small proof-of-concept application based on your needs and only after that go ahead and use it on your application.

You will now create a stand-alone application where you use the validator from an ordinary main method. In this example, you will define a new User bean and then validate an instance of this bean using rules that you define in an XML file and the implementation in Java code.

For this example, the validator rules are defined in a file named validate-bean.xml. This file defines a form and two validation rules that will be used to validate the form fields. The validator messages are defined in a file named validatorMsgs.properties and are accessed using java.util.ResourceBundle. Both validate-bean.xml and validatorMsgs.properties need to be present in the CLASSPATH for the code to access their contents. Listing 4-1 shows the contents of validatorMsgs.properties.

Listing 4-1. validatorMsgs.properties

```
nameForm.name = User Name
nameForm.age = User Age
err.checkRange = not in Range
err.required = is required
err.isInt = must be int
```

The validate-bean.xml file is where you have the validator configuration. Listing 4-2 shows the contents of this file. Considering that the validator comes from a Web application validation background, it works on the concepts of forms and fields. So even if you are validating the data in an instance of any class, you declare the validation rules in terms of forms and fields. So, as shown in Listing 4-2, even when you intend to validate the field values for an instance of a class, you have declared a form and two fields within the form.

Listing 4-2. `validate-bean.xml`

```
<form-validation>
    <global>
        <validator name="required"
            classname="com.commonsbook.chap4.ValidationTests"
            method="validateRequired"
            methodParams="java.lang.Object, org.apache.commons.validator.Field
                , java.util.HashMap, org.apache.commons.validator.ValidatorAction"
            msg="err.required"/>
        <validator name="isInt"
            classname="com.commonsbook.chap4.ValidationTests"
            method="validateInt"
            methodParams="java.lang.Object, org.apache.commons.validator.Field
                , java.util.HashMap, org.apache.commons.validator.ValidatorAction"
            msg="err.isInt"/>
        <validator name="checkRange"
            classname="com.commonsbook.chap4.ValidationTests"
            method="checkRange"
            methodParams="java.lang.Object, org.apache.commons.validator.Field
                , java.util.HashMap, org.apache.commons.validator.ValidatorAction"
            msg="err.checkRange"/>
    </global>
    <formset>
        <form name="nameForm">
            <field property="name" depends="required">
                <arg0 key="nameForm.name"/>
            </field>
            <field property="age" depends="isInt, checkRange">
                <arg0 key="nameForm.age"/>
                <var>
                    <var-name>max</var-name>
                    <var-value>30</var-value>
                </var>
                <var>
                    <var-name>min</var-name>
                    <var-value>20</var-value>
                </var>
            </field>
        </form>
    </formset>
</form-validation>
```

TIP *The* validate-bean.xml *file is special, but the filename is not. The filename can be anything you want. Also, you can change the names* isInt, checkRange, *and so on. The validator framework does not force a particular format for names of methods, classes, variables, and so on.*

This file defines the validation rules or validators, the method names, and the signatures that will actually have the logic for the validation and the classes that will contain these methods. This file and its contents are important because this file serves as the only medium through which you are communicating with the validator framework. You also define a form named nameForm whose properties name and age you will validate using the rules required and isInt, respectively. The validate-bean.xml file is conveying the following to the framework:

- The global tag will hold the elements that are meant to apply across all forms declared in the file.

- Within the global tag you declare a validator named required. You tell the framework that this validation will be performed by the validateRequired method in the class com.commonsbook.chap4.ValidationTests, and you define the four parameters that the method will expect. The msg attribute provides the key; using this key, an appropriate message will be picked from a properties file.

- You similarly declare two other validation rules named isInt and checkRange.

- Next you create a formset that is meant to hold multiple forms.

- You declare a single form named nameForm. This form has two fields named name and age.

- You use the depends attribute to tell the framework that the validation of the name field depends on the required validator and the validation of age depends on the two validators isInt and checkRange.

- The order in which validators are specified in the depends attribute is the order in which those rules are checked.

- For both fields you provide an argument named arg0, the key for which is a property name. You will use this property name to fetch the appropriate message from the properties file.

- To perform the checkRange validation, you require two variables that will tell you what the maximum and minimum values in the range are. These values are conveyed using the var tags.

Now that you have defined what will be validated and which classes and methods will do the actual validation, you will move on to the class whose instance you will be validating. The User bean whose instance you are validating is a basic class with two private fields and the corresponding get and set methods for these fields. Listing 4-3 shows the User bean class. Note that for each of the bean's properties, you have a field defined in the nameForm that you created in validate-bean.xml.

Listing 4-3. User *Class*

```
package com.commonsbook.chap4;
public class User {
    private String name;
    private String age;

    public User() {
    }

    public String getName() {
        return name;
    }

    public void setName(String newName) {
        name = newName;
    }

    public String getAge() {
        return age;
    }

    public void setAge(String newAge) {
        age = newAge;
    }
}
```

The ValidationTests class is where you define the methods that do the actual test for the validation. These methods are stated in the validation-bean.xml file, so you need to have a method signature matching those details. Nowhere in the code do you invoke the methods in the ValidationTests class. Because the framework does all method invocations, the signature stated in validate-bean.xml has to be strictly followed in the ValidationTests class.

The ValidationTests methods use the class org.apache.commons.validator. GenericValidator that provides various methods capable of checking most of the common validation cases. Because you will be storing validation-related messages in the validatorMsgs.properties file, to use that file, you need to use a ResourceBundle. This ResourceBundle is created static using the code in Listing 4-4 and is later used in all the validation methods.

Listing 4-4. Using validatorMsgs.properties *(*ValidationTests *Class)*

```
//ResourceBundle for Validator messages.
private static ResourceBundle valMsgsBundle = ResourceBundle.getBundle(
            "validatorMsgs");
```

You have already declared the validateRequired method in the validate-bean.xml file. Listing 4-5 shows the actual implementation of this method. Note that you are following the same method signature as stated in validate-bean.xml.

Listing 4-5. validateRequired *Method (*ValidationTests *Class)*

```
/**
* Validate required.
* @param bean The bean instance
* @param field The field being validated
* @param err HashMap that will hold validation errors
* @param va ValidatorAction
* @return if required value is provided true, else false
*/
public static boolean validateRequired(Object bean, Field field,
    HashMap err, org.apache.commons.validator.ValidatorAction va) {

    String value = ValidatorUtil.getValueAsString(bean, field.getProperty());
    String fieldName = valMsgsBundle.getString(field.getArg0().getKey());
    String actionMsg = valMsgsBundle.getString(va.getMsg());

    System.out.println("#### validateRequired value=" + value);

    if (GenericValidator.isBlankOrNull(value)) {
        System.out.println("validateRequired RETURN false");
        err.put(field.getKey(), fieldName + " " + actionMsg);
```

```
        return false;
    } else {
        System.out.println("validateRequired RETURN true");

        return true;
    }
}
```

In this method you first pick the value of the field using the getValueAsString method of the ValidatorUtil class and providing it with the bean instance and the name of the field. You next use the ResourceBundle created, as shown in Listing 4-4, and fetch the property values against the arg0 and msg attributes specified for the validateRequired method in the file validate-bean.xml.

You then use the isBlankOrNull method in the GenericValidator class to perform the actual validation. If the validation fails, you add a message to the HashMap that is meant to store all validation error messages. If validation is successful, the method returns true.

The next validation you have to perform is to check if a field value is int. The validateInt method as shown in Listing 4-6 does this task. The only real difference between the validateRequired and the validateInt methods is that here you use the isInt method of the GenericValidator class; in the case of validateRequired, you used the isBlankOrNull method.

Listing 4-6. validateInt Method (ValidationTests Class)

```
/**
* Validate int.
* @param bean The bean instance
* @param field The field being validated
* @param err HashMap that will hold validation errors
* @param va ValidatorAction
* @return if value is int true, else false
*/
public static boolean validateInt(Object bean, Field field,
    HashMap err, org.apache.commons.validator.ValidatorAction va) {

    String value = ValidatorUtil.getValueAsString(bean, field.getProperty());
    String fieldName = valMsgsBundle.getString(field.getArg0().getKey());
    String actionMsg = valMsgsBundle.getString(va.getMsg());
    System.out.println("#### validateInt value=" + value);

    if (GenericValidator.isInt(value)) {
        System.out.println("validateInt RETURN true");
```

```
        return true;
    } else {
        System.out.println("validateInt RETURN false");
        err.put(field.getKey(), fieldName + " " + actionMsg);

        return false;
    }
}
```

The last validation you have to perform is to check if the value provided is within a certain range. The checkRange method performs this task (see Listing 4-7).

Listing 4-7. checkRange *Method (*ValidationTests *Class)*

```
/**
 * Check Range.
 * @param bean The bean instance
 * @param field The field being validated
 * @param err HashMap that will hold validation errors
 * @param va ValidatorAction
 * @return if value is within range true, else false
 */
public static boolean checkRange(Object bean, Field field, HashMap err,
    org.apache.commons.validator.ValidatorAction va) {

    String value = ValidatorUtil.getValueAsString(bean, field.getProperty());
    String fieldName = valMsgsBundle.getString(field.getArg0().getKey());
    String actionMsg = valMsgsBundle.getString(va.getMsg());

    System.out.println("#### checkRange value=" + value);

    Var max = field.getVar("max");
    Var min = field.getVar("min");

    String maxVal = max.getValue();
    String minVal = min.getValue();

    if (GenericValidator.isInRange(Integer.parseInt(value),
            Integer.parseInt(minVal), Integer.parseInt(maxVal))) {
        System.out.println("checkRange RETURN true");
```

```
            return true;
        } else {
            System.out.println("checkRange RETURN false");
            err.put(field.getKey(), fieldName + " " + actionMsg);

            return false;
        }
    }
}
```

Here you use the `field` object to fetch the value of variables that have been specified in the `validate-bean.xml` file. When getting the `max` and `min` values, you use the `isInRange` method of the `GenericValidator` class to perform the validation. With this you are done writing the validators that will perform the validation. You now need to write the code that will use these validators.

> **NOTE** *As you will see from the methods, there is nothing that stops you from writing complex validation logic and creating new validation rules. You by no means are restricted to using just the* GenericValidator *class's validation capabilities. Define new validators in the* validate-bean.xml *file and provide implementation for the method, and you have your own validation logic plugged into the framework.*

The `ValidationTrial` class, as shown in Listing 4-8, is what triggers the validation as well as provides the bean to be validated. The method `validateMeth` is passed two arguments that are specified at runtime.

Listing 4-8. `ValidationTrial` *Class*

```
package com.commonsbook.chap4;
import org.apache.commons.validator.*;
import java.io.*;
import java.util.*;

public class ValidationTrial {
    public static void main(String[] args)
        throws IOException, ValidatorException {
        ValidationTrial validationTrial = new ValidationTrial();
        validationTrial.validateMeth(args[0], args[1]);
    }

    /**
     * The method that initializes and validates a User bean's fields.
```

```
 * @param age Age
 * @param name Name
 * @throws IOException
 * @throws ValidatorException
 */
public void validateMeth(String age, String name)
    throws IOException, ValidatorException {
    //Get Validator Configuration File as stream
    InputStream in = this.getClass().getClassLoader().getResourceAsStream(
            "validate-bean.xml");

    //Initialize ValidatorResourcess based on contents in validate-bean.xml
    ValidatorResources vRes = ValidatorResourcesInitializer.initialize(in);

    //Initialize a new bean. The contents of this bean will be validated.
    User uBean = new User();
    uBean.setAge(age);
    uBean.setName(name);

    //Create a new validator using
    //the initialized ValidatorResources and for form nameForm
    Validator val = new Validator(vRes, "nameForm");

    //Add to the validator the bean instance that is to be validated.
    val.addResource(Validator.BEAN_KEY, uBean);

    //Add HashMap as a resource where we will store all validation errors.
    HashMap err = new HashMap();
    val.addResource("java.util.HashMap", err);

    //Get Form from the ValidationResources.
    Form nForm = vRes.get(Locale.getDefault(), "nameForm");

    System.out.println("Validator actions >>>" +
        vRes.getValidatorActions());

    //Validate and get validation results.
    ValidatorResults valResults = val.validate();

    System.out.println("HashMap of validation errors >>>" +
        val.getResource("java.util.HashMap"));
}
}
```

The validateMeth method in Listing 4-8 performs the following steps:

1. Get an InputStream to the validate-bean.xml file.

2. Using the file, initialize ValidatorResources.

3. Create an instance of the bean and then set the values to be validated.

4. Create a new Validator instance using the ValidatorResources instance.

5. Add an instance of the User bean as a resource to the validator. This instance is what is being validated. You use Validator.BEAN_KEY as the key in this example.

6. Add the HashMap you will be using the store error messages. You add this HashMap as a resource to the Validator instance. It is important to specify the class name java.util.HashMap as the key.

7. Get the form nameForm. This step is not required, but I show it as something you can use if you need more information about the form being validated. You can invoke various methods on the form instance to get that information.

8. List the validator actions that will be performed.

9. Validate and get the results.

10. Get back the HashMap resource to check what errors have been inserted in the HashMap. The field names will be the key, and the messages will be the value.

Because you have used a HashMap to store validation errors, you have no use for the ValidatorResults object that is returned when calling the validate method. You can use this object to get more details of the validation results. You can iterate through all the fields for a form and every action for each form, picking up useful information while you iterate.

Note that the methods in the class ValidationTests get called automatically, and the returned boolean value of these methods is the deciding factor for a successful or failed validation. When executing this ValidationTrial code by passing the arguments ABC Boris, you will get the following output:

```
Validator actions >>>{checkRange=ValidatorAction: checkRange
, isInt=ValidatorAction: isInt
, required=ValidatorAction: required
}
```

```
#### validateRequired value=Boris
validateRequired RETURN true
#### validateInt value=ABC
validateInt RETURN false
HashMap of validation errors >>>{age=User Age must be int}
```

This output shows you that although the validateRequired validation succeeded and returned true, the validateInt method returned false because the value ABC that you passed is certainly not an int. Because the first rule for validating age was isInt, on its failure there was no need to check if the value is in a particular range. The errors HashMap holds the message User Age must be int. When running the program with arguments as 33 Boris, the output will be as follows:

```
Validator actions >>>{checkRange=ValidatorAction: checkRange
, isInt=ValidatorAction: isInt
, required=ValidatorAction: required
}
#### validateRequired value=Boris
validateRequired RETURN true
#### validateInt value=33
validateInt RETURN true
#### checkRange value=33
checkRange RETURN false
HashMap of validation errors >>>{age=User Age not in Range}
```

Here validateRequired and validateInt return true; however, because 33 does not lie within the range 20 to 30 that you have defined, that method returns false. The HashMap that holds the error messages also has the value User Age not in Range against the key age. Note that the actual message was created out of property values you picked from the validatorMsgs.properties file.

As you saw in this example, you can use the Validator component quite effectively to automate routine validations. Putting a new validation in place will take a little time up front, but you can consider it an investment that will bear rich dividends over the long term. Ideally you should keep building customized validations until you get to a stage where new development does not require that you write any new validations but just use the existing validations code and the Validator component to quickly get all validations for the application functioning.

Using the Struts Validator

Until recently, the validator was very much a tool meant only for using in tandem with the Struts framework. Although the validator was later moved to the Commons project and can be used independently of Struts, using it with Struts is how the validator is the most useful.

You will try out the validator as a part of Struts using Struts version 1.1. Struts 1.1 is quite a large download compared to version 1.0; you can find it at http://jakarta.apache.org/struts/. The binary download not only includes the requisite validator library but also includes Struts documentation and some examples in the form of Web Archive (WAR) files. The WAR files cannot only be easily deployed to any Java 2 Enterprise Edition (J2EE) server, but you could even just extract and use the Hypertext Markup Language (HTML) documentation files using any archiving tool such as WinZip, 7-Zip, and so on. The struts-validator.war file that is bundled with the Struts download can help you quickly understand how to use the validator in tandem with Struts. You will now create a simple validation example that is a bare-bones version of the struts-validator example you can find in the Struts download.

The application has a Java Server Page (JSP) that has a form that accepts user input. The validator you will create will check specific fields in the form for a few rules you define. If any of the validations fail, the reason for the error is displayed. If validation is successful, a new JSP containing a message is displayed.

I will go through the creation of this application one step at a time. I am presuming awareness of some basic Web application and Struts concepts. If you are involved in server-side Java and have not as yet used Struts, I certainly recommend you examine it. Struts is a useful and widely accepted framework that will help you build applications faster and in a systematic fashion.

The Web deployment descriptor (web.xml) needs to define a few things that are required by Struts. The web.xml file should be present in the WEB-INF directory and should have the contents shown in Listing 4-9.

Listing 4-9. Web Deployment Descriptor (web.xml)

```
<?xml version="1.0" encoding="ISO-8859-1"?>
<!DOCTYPE web-app
    PUBLIC "-//Sun Microsystems, Inc.//DTD Web Application 2.2//EN"
    "http://java.sun.com/j2ee/dtds/web-app_2_2.dtd">

<web-app>
    <display-name>Chapter 4 Validator Example</display-name>

    <!-- Action Servlet Configuration -->
    <servlet>
        <servlet-name>action</servlet-name>
        <servlet-class>org.apache.struts.action.ActionServlet</servlet-class>
        <init-param>
          <param-name>config</param-name>
          <param-value>/WEB-INF/struts-config.xml</param-value>
        </init-param>
        <load-on-startup>1</load-on-startup>
    </servlet>
```

```
<!-- Action Servlet Mapping -->
  <servlet-mapping>
      <servlet-name>action</servlet-name>
      <url-pattern>*.do</url-pattern>
  </servlet-mapping>

<!-- The Welcome File List -->
  <welcome-file-list>
      <welcome-file>index.jsp</welcome-file>
  </welcome-file-list>

<!-- Struts Tag Library Descriptors -->
  <taglib>
      <taglib-uri>/WEB-INF/struts-bean.tld</taglib-uri>
      <taglib-location>/WEB-INF/struts-bean.tld</taglib-location>
  </taglib>

  <taglib>
      <taglib-uri>/WEB-INF/struts-html.tld</taglib-uri>
      <taglib-location>/WEB-INF/struts-html.tld</taglib-location>
  </taglib>

  <taglib>
      <taglib-uri>/WEB-INF/struts-logic.tld</taglib-uri>
      <taglib-location>/WEB-INF/struts-logic.tld</taglib-location>
  </taglib>

</web-app>
```

The web.xml file does not define all the tag libraries provided by Struts but just the three tag libraries you intend to use. You also define a servlet named action that will act as the controller and map all requests in the format *.do to the action servlet.

Next you need to create a Struts ActionForm and Struts Action for the purpose of performing the validation and handling the flow of the application. You will define a single action and a single form. As shown in Listing 4-10, UserAction is a simple class that forwards the user to the appropriate page.

Listing 4-10. UserAction *Class*

```
package com.commonsbook.chap4;

import javax.servlet.http.HttpServletRequest;
import javax.servlet.http.HttpServletResponse;
```

```
import org.apache.struts.action.Action;
import org.apache.struts.action.ActionForm;
import org.apache.struts.action.ActionForward;
import org.apache.struts.action.ActionMapping;

public final class UserAction extends Action {

    public ActionForward execute(ActionMapping mapping,
    ActionForm form,
    HttpServletRequest request,
    HttpServletResponse response)
    throws Exception {

        UserForm user = (UserForm)form;
        return mapping.findForward("success");
    }
}
```

Because you intend to validate the values that the user submits as part of the
ActionForm, this form will extend org.apache.struts.validator.ValidatorForm.
Apart from that, as shown in Listing 4-11, it is just an ordinary class with three
fields that have corresponding get and set methods.

Listing 4-11. UserForm *Class*

```
package com.commonsbook.chap4;
import org.apache.struts.validator.ValidatorForm;

public final class UserForm extends ValidatorForm {

    private String firstName = null;
    private String lastName = null;
    private String email = null;

    public String getFirstName() {
        return firstName;
    }
    public void setFirstName(String firstName) {
        this.firstName = firstName;
    }
    public String getLastName() {
        return lastName;
```

```
        }
        public void setLastName(String lastName) {
            this.lastName = lastName;
        }
        public String getEmail() {
            return email;
        }
        public void setEmail(String email) {
            this.email = email;
        }
    }
}
```

Now that you have the action and the form created, you will define these in the Struts configuration file `struts-config.xml`. You name the form `userForm`, you name the action path `/userInfo`, and you also define a forward named `success` that will take the user to the page to be displayed when validation is successful. The `input` attribute of the `action` tag is important because this is the JSP that the user will be taken to if the validation fails. Listing 4-12 depicts the contents of the `struts-config.xml` file.

 NOTE *The* `message-resources` *tag specifies the properties file where the various application messages will be stored. Using a properties file for messages makes your application customization and changes a lot easier and does not require any change to existing code.*

Listing 4-12. `struts-config.xml`

```
<?xml version="1.0" encoding="ISO-8859-1" ?>
<!DOCTYPE struts-config PUBLIC
        "-//Apache Software Foundation//DTD Struts Configuration 1.1//EN"
        "http://jakarta.apache.org/struts/dtds/struts-config_1_1.dtd">

<struts-config>
  <!--Forms -->
    <form-beans>
        <!-- User Information form -->
        <form-bean name="userForm" type="com.commonsbook.chap4.UserForm"/>
    </form-beans>
```

```
   <!--Actions -->
     <action-mappings>
         <action      path="/userInfo"
                       type="com.commonsbook.chap4.UserAction"
                       name="userForm"
                       scope="request"
                       validate="true"
                       input="/index.jsp">
             <forward name="success" path="/done.jsp"/>
         </action>
     </action-mappings>

   <!-- Message Resources to be used-->
   <message-resources parameter="com.commonsbook.chap4.ApplicationResources"/>

   <!--Define Validator Plug Ins-->
     <plug-in className="org.apache.struts.validator.ValidatorPlugIn">
         <set-property property="pathnames" value="/WEB-INF/validation.xml"/>
     </plug-in>
</struts-config>
```

Next you need to create two JSPs, one where the user enters the data and the second to display the message if validation is successful. The index.jsp file uses the tag libraries you defined in the web.xml file. The HTML tag library provides dynamic alternatives to the standard HTML tags. Based on the key specified, the bean:message tag picks up the message from the message resource specified in the struts-config.xml file.

NOTE   *The Struts tag libraries make JSP development systematic and your code a lot cleaner. The JSP Standard Tag Libraries (JSTL) are also a good, standardized alternative. It is well worth investing the time required to learn these tag libraries. You can find the JSTL specification at* http://java.sun.com/products/jstl/. *You can find Jakarta Taglibs, which is the reference implementation for the specification, at* http://jakarta.apache.org/taglibs/.

Listing 4-13 shows index.jsp.

Listing 4-13. index.jsp

```
<%@ page language="java" %>
<%@ taglib uri="/WEB-INF/struts-bean.tld" prefix="bean" %>
<%@ taglib uri="/WEB-INF/struts-html.tld" prefix="html" %>
```

```
<%@ taglib uri="/WEB-INF/struts-logic.tld" prefix="logic" %>
<html:html>
<head>
<title>Validator Trial</title>
<html:base/>
</head>
<body bgcolor="white">
    <logic:messagesPresent>
        <bean:message key="errors.header"/>
        <ul>
        <html:messages id="error">
            <li><bean:write name="error"/></li>
        </html:messages>
        </ul><hr>
    </logic:messagesPresent>
    <html:form action="userInfo">
        <table border="0" width="60%">
          <tr>
            <th align="left">
              <bean:message key="firstname.display"/>
            </th>
            <td align="left">
              <html:text property="firstName" size="20"/>
            </td>
          </tr>
          <tr>
            <th align="left">
              <bean:message key="lastname.display"/>
            </th>
            <td align="left">
              <html:text property="lastName" size="20"/>
            </td>
          </tr>
          <tr>
            <th align="left">
              <bean:message key="email.display"/>
            </th>
            <td align="left">
              <html:text property="email" size="40"/>
            </td>
          </tr>
```

```
          <tr>
            <td>
              <html:submit property="submit">
                  Submit
              </html:submit>
               
              <html:reset>
                  Reset
              </html:reset>
            </td>
          </tr>
        </table>
    </html:form>
</body>
</html:html>
```

In this piece of code, the tag to note is the `logic:messagesPresent` tag and its child tags. When `index.jsp` is invoked for the first time, the `logic:messagesPresent` tag does not come into action because no messages are present. However, if validation on form submission fails, you direct the user back to this same page. In this case, the reasons for the validation's failure are present as messages, and courtesy of the `logic:messagesPresent` tag, these messages get displayed. The `html:messages` tag iterates through the messages, and the `bean:write` tag displays the actual message. You can also use the tag `html:errors` to display error message associated with a particular field.

Running the Application

Before you get into the part that the validator plays in this application, you will first look at what results you can expect. To run the application, all you need is to create a Web application in the standard J2EE structure. Place the class files and the `ApplicationResources.properties` files in the `WEB-INF/classes` directory, and place `struts.jar` and other JARs that Struts and the Validator component depend on in the `WEB-INF/lib` directory. The two JSPs are placed at the top level in the application's structure.

To run this application on Jakarta Tomcat 4.*x*, all you have to do is place the Web application directory into Tomcat's `webapps` directory and then start the server. For this example, I named the directory `validatorStrutsApp` and placed this directory in the `webapps` directory. The URL `http://localhost:8080/validatorStrutsApp` will display the `index.jsp` page on your screen, as shown in Figure 4-1.

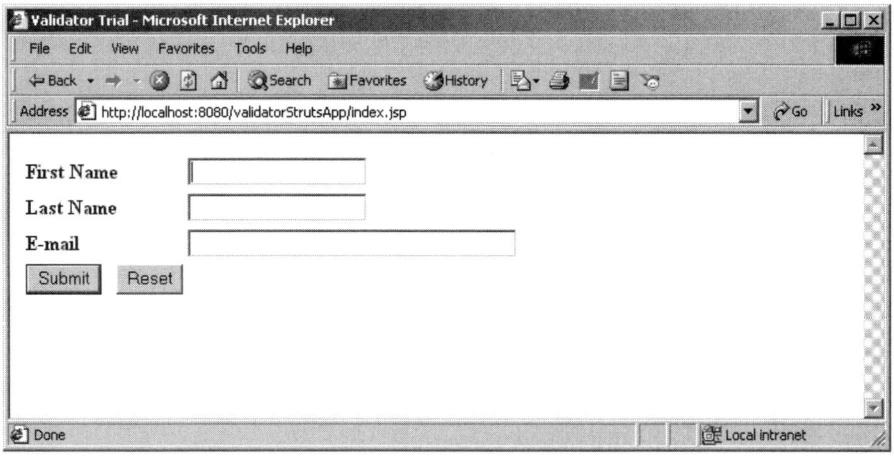

Figure 4-1. index.jsp *user input form*

Based on how many validations fail, the appropriate error messages are displayed using the html:messages tag. In this example, if the user clicks the Submit button without entering any data, the screen shown in Figure 4-2 will display. If all validations are successful, you forward the user to the done.jsp screen, as shown in Figure 4-3.

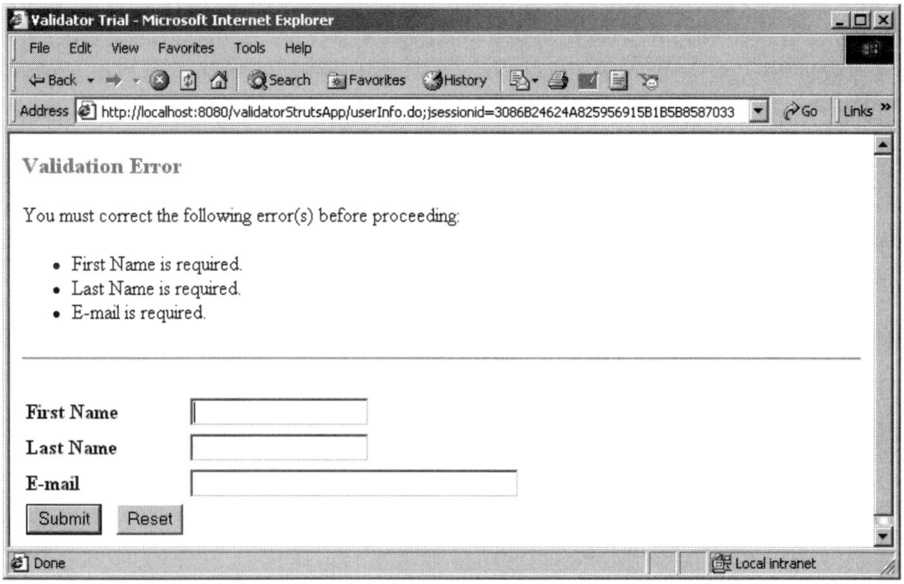

Figure 4-2. Validation errors display

Figure 4-3. No validation error; form submit successful

Validator Components

Now that you know what you want to achieve, you will look the validation-related components and the parts they play. You have already looked at some of these components in the "Using the Validator Independently" section.

The struts-config file is a key resource for managing how Struts works. So the first thing you need to do if you want to integrate the validator with Struts is to define the plug-in tag in the struts-config file. As shown in the struts-config file you saw in Listing 4-4, the plug-in tag needs to be told the class name for the plug-in; you can also set properties for purposes specific to the plug-in being used. In this example, you set a property named pathnames to tell the validator plug-in the location to look for the validator configuration file. You can specify multiple files by separating the paths with a comma. In this example, you convey that /WEB-INF/validation.xml is the file where all validation-related configuration information resides. Now you will look at what purpose the validation.xml file serves in the validator scheme of things.

validation.xml

With Struts or without it, this file is the core of the validator. This is where you define validation methods, constants, forms, form fields, and the validations to be performed on individual fields. The convention is to name the file that has validations for the application as validation.xml and have a separate file named validation-rules.xml. This is not compulsory, and you can merge the contents of the two files into a single file as in this example. Listing 4-14 shows the validation.xml file for this example.

Listing 4-14. `validation.xml`

```
<?xml version="1.0" encoding="ISO-8859-1" ?>


<!DOCTYPE form-validation PUBLIC
"-//Apache Software Foundation//DTD Commons Validator Rules Configuration 1.0//EN"
"http://jakarta.apache.org/commons/dtds/validator_1_0.dtd">
<form-validation>
    <global>
        <validator name="required"
              classname="org.apache.struts.validator.FieldChecks"
                  method="validateRequired"
            methodParams="java.lang.Object,
                          org.apache.commons.validator.ValidatorAction,
                          org.apache.commons.validator.Field,
                          org.apache.struts.action.ActionErrors,
                          javax.servlet.http.HttpServletRequest"
                    msg="errors.required">
        </validator>

        <validator name="email"
              classname="org.apache.struts.validator.FieldChecks"
                  method="validateEmail"
            methodParams="java.lang.Object,
                          org.apache.commons.validator.ValidatorAction,
                          org.apache.commons.validator.Field,
                          org.apache.struts.action.ActionErrors,
                          javax.servlet.http.HttpServletRequest"
                depends=""
                    msg="errors.email">
        </validator>
    </global>
    <formset>
        <form     name="userForm">
            <field     property="firstName"
                  depends="required">
                    <arg0 key="firstname.display"/>
            </field>
            <field     property="lastName"
                  depends="required">
                    <arg0 key="lastname.display"/>
            </field>
```

```
            <field    property="email"
                  depends="required,email">
                    <arg0 key="email.display"/>
            </field>
        </form>
    </formset>
</form-validation>
```

Now you will look at each of the important tags in validation.xml, beginning with the tag that defines the validations, the validator tag.

The validator Tag

The first tag to note is the validator tag. In each validator tag you specify the attributes classname and method. These attributes tell the validator which Java method actually has the logic for the validations.

 NOTE *The Struts-specific validator classes such as* org.apache.struts.validator.FieldChecks *are part of* struts.jar *and are not found in the* commons-validator.jar *file.*

For the required validation rule that you have defined, you tell the validator to invoke the method validateRequired of the class org.apache.struts.validator. FieldChecks. You next tell the validator to pass the four parameters to this method. The message tag defines the key value in the message resource you are using. So if an error occurs in the required validation, the message corresponding to the key errors.required will be used.

The email validation is also defined on a similar line. Only the attribute values for method and key are changed.

Once you use the validator tags to tell the validator framework that you want to use the required and email validation rules, you need to specify the forms to be validated using these. The formset tag can hold multiple forms using independent form tags.

The form Tag

In the index.jsp page, you have defined three input fields in a HTML form named userForm. You also have defined this form in struts-config under the same name. For validation to be performed on this form, you saw in Listing 4-3 that the form class needs to extend the ValidatorForm class. Apart from that requirement, you also need to define the form and the fields you want to validate in the validation.xml file.

In this example, you define a new form named userForm. This name has to be the same as defined in struts-config. In this form you have the option of validating only a few fields and not the entire form. For this example, the field validations are as shown in Table 4-2.

Table 4-2. userForm *Field Validations*

Name	Validations	MessageKey
firstName	required	firstname.display
lastName	required	lastname.display
email	required	email.display
	email	email.display

The depends attribute value for the form field tags can be any of the name attribute values of the various validator tags you have defined. So, for this example, validation of any form field can depend on required and email validators. If multiple rules are to be applied, a comma is used to separate the validator names.

That is all you need to do to have the Validator component validate form submissions in a Struts application. When the form is submitted, based on the rules you have specified in the validation.xml file, the appropriate validation methods get called. If any validations fail, error keys are returned, and based on these keys, the corresponding message from the message resource is picked up from the message resource defined in struts-config.xml. As shown in Figure 4-2, the JSP, with the help of some Struts custom tags, then displays messages for all the validations that failed.

Once you get the hang of validator usage in tandem with Struts, developing and maintaining validations is quite simple. The savings on bug fixing and customization time is also an important advantage.

Summary

In this chapter you used the Validator component in tandem with Struts and as an independent component. The validator is a handy tool and has proven to be so especially in the Struts Web application world. I certainly recommend you use the validator for Struts applications.

If you are building small applications, it might not always be worth the effort to build the Validator component into the application. However, as a long-term strategy, it is a wise move to use the validator extensively on projects so you can keep building and reusing new validations specific to your kind of development.

CHAPTER 5

Using the BeanUtils Component

A LOT OF TODAY'S APPLICATIONS use JavaBeans. These beans do nothing smart but are primarily meant to move data around in a systematic format. I am using the term *JavaBeans* in a rather narrow sense. I mean simple Java classes adhering to the JavaBeans naming pattern that have a few fields and corresponding get and set methods. Their use is rampant, and most applications are full of these classes. They might be used as value objects, Struts ActionForm objects, and so on, but their purposes remain almost the same. These classes move data, in most cases using private variables with read and write access provided by the appropriate get and set methods.

The BeanUtils component is an attempt to make working with these classes simpler and more systematic. The component not only provides utility classes that can handle a lot of the mundane tasks associated with these beans but also provides functionality to eliminate the need to manually create these classes. Another important place where you can use BeanUtils is when you are not aware of the class to be used or the property whose value is to be fetched. If these decisions will be made at runtime, your code needs to be dynamic enough to handle the situation. BeanUtils can do that for you.

For the record, the BeanUtils component is known as the Bean Introspection Utilities. The word *introspection* makes it sound high-tech and difficult to adopt, but that is certainly not the case. The BeanUtils component has its origins in the Struts framework and plays an important part in how Struts works. However, it is also useful for applications that have nothing to do with Struts. A good thing about the BeanUtils component is that the Javadocs are to the point and contain many usage examples. You can find the JavaBeans specification at http://java.sun.com/javabeans/docs/spec.html. Table 5-1 shows the component details.

Table 5-1. Component Details

Name	Version	Package
BeanUtils	1.6.1	org.apache.commons.beanutils

Ringing Out the Old...Ringing In the New

In this chapter, I demonstrate how the BeanUtils component can help you streamline your Java code and get rid of a lot of helper code that on its own does not do much. BeanUtils can help you eliminate the need for having many data object classes that only hold data and move it around. BeanUtils can also help you implement a consistent methodology for accessing all JavaBeans. An important advantage of BeanUtils is that the properties of your beans and the code that uses the beans are not locked into your code and the exact property names and method signatures. With BeanUtils, you can dynamically (or based on some runtime input) change the property name or usage.

You can download the BeanUtils component at http://jakarta.apache.org/ commons/beanutils/. BeanUtils depends on the following packages, so you need to download these before you can use BeanUtils:

- The Collections package (Jakarta Commons), version 1.0 or later

- The Logging package (Jakarta Commons), version 1.0 or later

A quick example should illustrate the relevance and use of the BeanUtils component. Do not worry too much about the methods and classes involved. The purpose of the example is solely to highlight the benefits of using BeanUtils-based code instead of standard Java code. You will first look at the traditional bean code and then the BeanUtils-based code. In this example, all you want to achieve is to instantiate a bean, set one of its property values, and then fetch that value.

Listing 5-1 shows the traditional code to serve this purpose.

Listing 5-1. OldBeanUsage *Class*

```
package com.commonsbook.chap5;
public class OldBeanUsage {
    public static void main(String[] args) {
        //Instantiate bean
        TheBean bean = new TheBean();

        //Set property value
        bean.setAField("VALUE");

        //Get property value
        System.out.println("AField = " + bean.getAField());
    }
}
```

```
/**
 * Define a separate class for the bean
 */
class TheBean {
    private String aField;

    public TheBean() {
    }

    public String getAField() {
        return aField;
    }

    public void setAField(String newAField) {
        aField = newAField;
    }
}
```

In this piece of code, you instantiate a class named TheBean, set the value of a field, and then get back that value. The output on execution is AField = VALUE.

Now you will look at the BeanUtils alternative. It is unlikely that you will understand how exactly the code works, but try to just get a feel for the code. I will delve into specifics later in the chapter. The piece of code shown in Listing 5-2 achieves the same functionality as Listing 5-1.

Listing 5-2. NewBeanUsage *Class*

```
package com.commonsbook.chap5;
import org.apache.commons.beanutils.BasicDynaClass;
import org.apache.commons.beanutils.DynaBean;
import org.apache.commons.beanutils.DynaProperty;
import org.apache.commons.beanutils.PropertyUtils;

public class NewBeanUsage {
    public static void main(String[] args) throws Exception {
        //Define properties for the dynamic class
        DynaProperty[] props = new DynaProperty[] {
                new DynaProperty("aField", java.lang.String.class)
            };

        //Define the class
        BasicDynaClass dynaClass = new BasicDynaClass("AnotherBean", null, props);
```

```
//Instantiate the class
DynaBean dBean = dynaClass.newInstance();

//Set property value
PropertyUtils.setSimpleProperty(dBean, "aField", "VALUE");

//Get property value
System.out.println("AField = " +
    PropertyUtils.getSimpleProperty(dBean, "aField"));
    }
}
```

When comparing the two bits of code, the obvious change is that with the BeanUtils code, you do not need to write the class TheBean that you see in Listing 5-1 or define its properties and their corresponding getter and setter methods. Also, in the BeanUtils code you have the advantage of defining and using a bean right within a single piece of code with no need for a separate class. You have not achieved a drastic reduction in code size, and the BeanUtils code is also a little tougher to comprehend than the old code; however, consider the following:

How would the two blocks of code react if the number of properties went up to, say, 20? Although the BeanUtils code would see an addition of only 19 new instances of DynaProperty, the old code size would explode. You would have to define 19 new properties in the TheBean class and new getter and setter methods for each property.

Is the code locked into a definite class? The old code certainly is because the properties—along with the getter and setter methods—are stated in the class TheBean, which needs to be explicitly instantiated to make the calls on the getter and setter methods. The BeanUtils code does not define any such class, so the code is perfectly flexible. You could have easily passed the name, type, and number of properties as runtime arguments.

How many classes do you have to maintain? I am not aware of any statistics to prove the point, but I do think that every new class introduced will add significantly to the time and effort involved in maintaining an application. In Listing 5-2 you got rid of the class TheBean that existed in Listing 5-1, so you have one less class to maintain.

Are your property names locked in? Again, with the old code, they are. Just renaming a property can cause a lot of problems and rework. With the BeanUtils code, no method name is based on a property name. Property names are parameters, and changing them is simple.

The BeanUtils approach has many such advantages that make it a flexible and useful offering. If you want to use BeanUtils to access an existing bean, the precondition is that the bean class should be public and have a default no-arguments constructor. This is required so you can instantiate the class without knowing its name by using the newInstance method of the class java.lang.Class. The BeanUtils component uses the get and set methods that adhere to the JavaBeans naming standard. If you want to use an existing bean that has a boolean property, you have the option of naming the getXxx method as well as isXxx. So instead of having a method getAdult, you can have a method named isAdult and still use BeanUtils to get the property value. To use method names not adhering to the getXxx and setXxx format, you have the option of specifying the format using the BeanInfo class associated with the bean.

 NOTE *The fields in a class are often referred to as* variables, fields, members, *and so on almost interchangeably. However, with BeanUtils, the preferred word is* properties.

Property access and dynamic beans are the two major features of the BeanUtils package. You will now look at how BeanUtils categorizes properties and how these are accessed using the utility classes provided.

Understanding Property Types

The BeanUtils component splits properties into four types:

Simple property: A *simple property* is where the property value itself is the value you want to get or set. It can be a primitive type, a Java class, or even a user-defined class. The distinguishing factor is that you do not intend to go a level into the property and fetch a value within.

Indexed property: An *indexed property* is any property that is an ordered collection of objects where all objects are of the same type and each object can be individually accessed by an integer-valued, non-negative index. An array, ArrayList, and Vector are all examples of indexed properties. Having said that, if you are not using dynamic beans and are using a standard JavaBean, BeanUtils does not require that you have an ArrayList or a Vector as a property. You will learn about dynamic beans (also known as DynaBeans) later in this chapter. BeanUtils will work fine even if the appropriate getXxx (int index) and setXxx (int index, Foo foo) methods exist and no property Xxx is actually present. Using an index to get or set a value is integral to using indexed properties.

Mapped property: A *mapped property* is of type java.util.Map, and the collection of data is in the form of key/value pairs. You have to use a key to get or set the value of a mapped property. Similarly to indexed properties, again BeanUtils does not require that you have a Map as a property. BeanUtils will work fine even if the appropriate getXxx (String key) and setXxx(String key, Foo foo) methods are present, and it will not care if a property Xxx exists.

Nested property: A *nested property* is a property within a property. To access a nested property, you first have to fetch one property, and from within that property you fetch a second property.

You will now look at a comprehensive example that will use all these types of properties. You are not using dynamic beans for this example, so first you need to create the beans that will serve as the basis for the property access.

This bean holds some data about a person. This data is represented in the form of private properties that can be accessed through public getter and setter methods. For each of these properties there is a public get and set method. Because the class does nothing important and yet stretches into more than 100 lines, I will include only small portions of the code. The properties in the class Person are as follows:

```
private String name; //Simple property
private int age; //Simple property
private HashMap phoneNumbers; //Mapped property
private Computer homeComputer; //Simple property
private Computer workComputer; //Simple property
private String[] pastEmployers; // Indexed property
private ArrayList certifications; //Indexed property
```

You will be storing more details about the computers used by the person in a separate class named Computer. This class has the following properties and the corresponding getter and setter methods:

```
private String processor;
private String ramDetails;
private String adminUser;
private String operatingSystem;
```

You will now use the property access capabilities of the BeanUtils component to set these properties and then access them. In this example shown in Listing 5-3, you will use all the four properties types: simple, indexed, mapped, and nested.

NOTE *You cannot directly set values against an index in a list. This is possible only if an object already exists in the list at that index and you want to replace it with a new object. That is why you first created a* certifications ArrayList *before you set or get values from it.*

Listing 5-3. BeanUtilsPersonTrial *Class*

```
package com.commonsbook.chap5;
import org.apache.commons.beanutils.PropertyUtils;

import java.util.ArrayList;
import java.util.HashMap;

public class BeanUtilsPersonTrial {
    public static void main(String[] args) throws Exception {
        //Initialize new Person
        Person p = new Person();

        //Set simple properties
        PropertyUtils.setSimpleProperty(p, "name", "Mr. X");
        PropertyUtils.setSimpleProperty(p, "age", new Integer(30));

        PropertyUtils.setSimpleProperty(p, "pastEmployers",
            new String[] { "Microsoft", "Sun", "IBM" });

        //ArrayList of certifications
        ArrayList cert = new ArrayList();
        cert.add("SCJP");
        cert.add("SCWCD");

        PropertyUtils.setSimpleProperty(p, "certifications", cert);

        PropertyUtils.setSimpleProperty(p, "phoneNumbers", new HashMap());
        PropertyUtils.setSimpleProperty(p, "homeComputer", new Computer());
        PropertyUtils.setSimpleProperty(p, "workComputer", new Computer());

        //Set string at index 0 in array
        PropertyUtils.setIndexedProperty(p, "pastEmployers", 0, "BEA");
        PropertyUtils.setIndexedProperty(p, "certifications", 1, "SCEA");
```

```
//Set mapped properties
PropertyUtils.setMappedProperty(p, "phoneNumbers", "home", "111222333");
PropertyUtils.setMappedProperty(p, "phoneNumbers", "office", "00000000");

//Set mapped properties
PropertyUtils.setNestedProperty(p, "homeComputer.processor", "Intel P4");
PropertyUtils.setNestedProperty(p, "homeComputer.ramDetails", "512 MB");
PropertyUtils.setNestedProperty(p, "homeComputer.operatingSystem",
    "Win2K");

System.out.println("***Simple Property Access***");
System.out.println("\tSimpProp name= " +
    PropertyUtils.getSimpleProperty(p, "name"));
System.out.println("\tSimpProp age= " +
    PropertyUtils.getSimpleProperty(p, "age"));

System.out.println("***Mapped Property Access***");
System.out.println("\tMapProp phoneNumbers > home= " +
    PropertyUtils.getMappedProperty(p, "phoneNumbers", "home"));
System.out.println("\tMapProp phoneNumbers > office= " +
    PropertyUtils.getMappedProperty(p, "phoneNumbers(office)"));

System.out.println("***Indexed Property Access***");
System.out.println("\tIndProp pastEmployers[0] = " +
    PropertyUtils.getIndexedProperty(p, "pastEmployers", 0));
System.out.println("\tIndProp certifications[1] = " +
    PropertyUtils.getIndexedProperty(p, "certifications[1]"));

System.out.println("***Nested Property Access***");
System.out.println("\tNestedProperty homeComputer.processor = " +
    PropertyUtils.getNestedProperty(p, "homeComputer.processor"));
System.out.println("\tNestedProperty homeComputer.ramDetails = " +
    PropertyUtils.getNestedProperty(p, "homeComputer.ramDetails"));
System.out.println("\tNestedProperty homeComputer.operatingSystem = " +
    PropertyUtils.getNestedProperty(p, "homeComputer.operatingSystem"));

System.out.println("***Other Utilities***");
System.out.println("Describe the object: \n" +
    PropertyUtils.describe(p));
System.out.println("homeComputer.adminUser Readable = " +
    PropertyUtils.isReadable(p, "homeComputer.adminUser"));
System.out.println("homeComputer.adminUser Writable = " +
    PropertyUtils.isWriteable(p, "homeComputer.adminUser"));

    }
}
```

In this piece of code, you have just set the various property values using the setXxx methods provided by the PropertyUtils class and then fetched those values using the getXxx methods of the PropertyUtils class. Try to relate the setXxx usage and the corresponding getXxx usage to understand how and from where a certain property value is being fetched. The output upon executing this code is as follows:

```
***Simple Property Access***
        SimpProp name= Mr. X
        SimpProp age= 30
***Mapped Property Access***
        MapProp phoneNumbers > home= 111222333
        MapProp phoneNumbers > office= 00000000
***Indexed Property Access***
        IndProp pastEmployers[0] = BEA
        IndProp certifications[1] = SCEA
***Nested Property Access***
        NestedProperty homeComputer.processor = Intel P4
        NestedProperty homeComputer.ramDetails = 512 MB
        NestedProperty homeComputer.operatingSystem = Win2K
***Other Utilities***
Describe the object:
{phoneNumbers={office=00000000, home=111222333}, age=30, name=Mr. X
, pastEmployers=[Ljava.lang.String;@5, workComputer=
com.commonsbook.chap5.Computer@6, class=class com.commonsbook.chap5.Person
, certifications=[SCJP, SCEA], homeComputer=com.commonsbook.chap5.Computer@7}
homeComputer.adminUser Readable = true
homeComputer.adminUser Writable = false
```

Other than getter and setter methods, for indexed properties you have another option that BeanUtils can use to get the value at a particular index. You need to do a little additional work and provide additional getter and setter methods in the Person class. You have to provide these methods to be able to get objects from a specific index and to set objects at a specific index.

You have to provide the additional getter and setter methods for the properties pastEmployers and certifications because these are the properties you will be accessing using the indexed property capability of PropertyUtils. These methods are as follows:

```
public String getPastEmployers(int index) {
    return (pastEmployers[index]);
}
```

```
public void setPastEmployers(int index, String value) {
    pastEmployers[index] = value;
}

public String getCertifications(int index) {
    return (String)certifications.get(index);
}

public void setCertifications(int index, String value) {
    certifications.set(index, value);
}
```

These methods get automatically called based on the parameters provided to the getIndexedProperty and setIndexedProperty methods of PropertyUtils. While trying to use these new methods to access a certification at an index, I faced some unexpected errors saying Property 'certifications' has no setter method. I resolved this issue by getting rid of the setCertifications method in the Person class, and instead of setting the certifications ArrayList in BeanUtilsTrial, I initialized the ArrayList in the Person class. I also had to comment out the following line in the BeanUtilsTrial:

```
PropertyUtils.setSimpleProperty(p, "certifications", cert);
```

Apart from the property access functionality, the isReadable and isWriteable methods also can be quite useful if you are uncertain of the access provided to a certain property. Also note the two different method signatures used while accessing mapped and indexed properties.

The describe method serves to quickly fetch all properties and their values and is especially useful while debugging applications.

Now that you have seen most of the property setting and getting functionality of PropertyUtils, you will look closer at a special feature of BeanUtils, dynamic beans, or DynaBeans.

Using Dynamic Beans

As the name suggests, *dynamic beans* provide dynamism and energy to otherwise routine and boring tasks. DynaBeans are the reason why with Struts 1.1 creating your own ActionForm classes is not always required. DynaBeans can also make access to database ResultSet and RowSet objects many times more systematic than getting values based on the column number in the query.

You can call dynamic beans *autogenerated beans,* which, based on their configuration, consist of the properties required as well as the corresponding getter and setter methods. You saw a simple example in Listing 5-2 where you created a DynaBean that consisted of a single property. I will now delve into the various interfaces and classes involved and the functionality they offer.

The two interfaces that form the key to DynaBean functionality are DynaBean and DynaClass. While DynaClass is meant to represent the class you want to instantiate, DynaBean represents the actual instance of that class. You will now have a closer look at DynaClass and its various types.

The DynaClass interface provides the basic features expected from a class for it to be instantiated and used. Four classes—BasicDynaClass, ResultSetDynaClass, RowSetDynaClass, and WrapDynaClass—implement the DynaClass interface. You will now look at each of these.

BasicDynaClass

This class provides bare minimum functionality but is still good enough for most requirements. A handy and simple-to-use class, it can also serve as a base class for any complex implementations you might want to provide. However, it is unlikely that you would need to write your own customized implementation.

The three constructors for this class give you the option to create a class while specifying the properties or the DynaBean implementation to be used. You will look at an example where you create a BasicDynaClass that has a single ArrayList property. Listing 5-4 shows the code for the class.

Listing 5-4. BasicDynaTrial *Class*

```
package com.commonsbook.chap5;
import org.apache.commons.beanutils.BasicDynaBean;
import org.apache.commons.beanutils.BasicDynaClass;
import org.apache.commons.beanutils.DynaBean;
import org.apache.commons.beanutils.DynaProperty;
import org.apache.commons.beanutils.PropertyUtils;

import java.util.ArrayList;

public class BasicDynaTrial {
    public static void main(String[] args) throws Exception {
        //Define properties for the dynamic class
        DynaProperty[] props = new DynaProperty[] {
                new DynaProperty("arPropOne", ArrayList.class)
            };
```

```
        //ArrayList meant to be set as a property
        ArrayList arObjs = new ArrayList();
        arObjs.add("OBJ1");
        arObjs.add("OBJ2");

        //Define the class
        BasicDynaClass basicDynaClass = new BasicDynaClass("BasicBean", null,
                props);

        //Instantiate the class
        DynaBean dBean = basicDynaClass.newInstance();

        //Another way to instantiate a BasicDynaBean
        BasicDynaBean basicDB = new BasicDynaBean(basicDynaClass);

        //Set property value
        PropertyUtils.setSimpleProperty(dBean, "arPropOne", arObjs);

        //Get Property value
        System.out.println("[dBean] ArrayList arObjs = " +
            PropertyUtils.getSimpleProperty(dBean, "arPropOne"));

        //Get Indexed Property value
        System.out.println("[dBean] arObjs[1] = " +
            PropertyUtils.getIndexedProperty(dBean, "arPropOne", 1));
    }
}
```

You create an instance of BasicDynaBean using the BasicDynaClass that you create. You have the option of creating the bean either by using the newInstance method of the BasicDynaClass class or by directly instantiating a BasicDynaBean and providing the BasicDynaClass as a parameter to its constructor.

In Listing 5-4, you could very well have provided the object basicDB instead of the object dBean to the PropertyUtils method calls, and you would have gotten this same output:

```
[dBean] ArrayList arObjs = [OBJ1, OBJ2]
[dBean] arObjs[1] = OBJ2
```

ResultSetDynaClass

ResultSetDynaClass is a subclass of DynaClass meant specifically to handle java.sql.ResultSet. Anyone familiar with Java Database Connectivity (JDBC) will appreciate that ResultSet objects are not the easiest things to work with, and often projects resort to filling up beans with ResultSet data and then using those beans.

ResultSetDynaClass provides a better alternative because a bean with properties that map with the columns fetched in the ResultSet can be created automatically. You can then use this bean easily with the PropertyUtils methods you have been using throughout this chapter.

 CAUTION   *The* DynaBean *created based on the* ResultSet *refers to the objects in the* ResultSet. *So you still need to be well aware of the current position in the* ResultSet *to which you are referring. If the* ResultSet *gets closed, the* DynaBean *cannot be used anymore.*

You will now see an example where ResultSetDynaClass is used. For this example, I am using a database named test running on my local machine on port 3306. The database contains a single table named User (see Table 5-2). The User table has three fields named UserId, UserName, and Age. Age is an int, and the other two columns are varchar. To execute this example on a MySQL database, you have to download the MySQL JDBC driver from http://www.mysql.com/.

Table 5-2. User *Table Contents*

UserId	UserName	Age
1	X	20
2	Y	30
3	Z	40

Listing 5-5 shows the code to fetch this data and access it using ResultSetDynaClass.

Listing 5-5. ResultSetDynaTrial *Class*

```
package com.commonsbook.chap5;
import java.sql.*;
import java.util.*;
import org.apache.commons.beanutils.*;
```

```java
public class ResultSetDynaTrial {
    public static void main(String[] args) {
        Connection con =null;
        Statement st =null;
        ResultSet rs =null;

        try {
            //Class.forName("sun.jdbc.odbc.JdbcOdbcDriver");
            //String url="jdbc:odbc:BeanUtilsDB";
            Class.forName("com.mysql.jdbc.Driver");
            String url="jdbc:mysql://127.0.0.1:3306/test";
            con = DriverManager.getConnection(url,"", "");
            st= con.createStatement();
            rs= st.executeQuery(
            "SELECT UserName as uName, AgE FROM USER"
            );
            ResultSetDynaClass rsDynaClass= new ResultSetDynaClass(rs);
            Iterator itr= rsDynaClass.iterator();

            while(itr.hasNext()) {
                DynaBean dBean= (DynaBean)itr.next();
                System.out.println("username "
                    +PropertyUtils.getSimpleProperty(dBean, "uname"));
                System.out.println("age "
                    +PropertyUtils.getSimpleProperty(dBean, "age"));
                //System.out.println(PropertyUtils.describe(dBean));
            }
        }
        catch(Exception e) {
            e.printStackTrace();
        }
        finally {
            try {
                if(rs!=null) { rs.close(); }
                if(st!=null) { st.close(); }
                if(con!=null) { con.close(); }
            }
            catch(Exception e) { e.printStackTrace(); }
        }
    }
}
```

NOTE   *Regardless of the case used while stating the column names, the property name provided to the* PropertyUtils *method has to be lowercase.*

NOTE   *In the SQL query, instead of stating all the column names, you can use aliases for column names as well as the * operator.*

The output upon executing the code shown in Listing 5-5 is as follows:

```
username X
age 20
username Y
age 30
username Z
age 40
```

ResultSetDynaClass thus makes accessing JDBC ResultSet objects a lot more systematic. However, ResultSetDynaClass still suffers from some of the flaws of the underlying ResultSet being used, and the bean cannot be used and transported independently of the status of the ResultSet. RowSetDynaClass is meant to solve this problem.

RowSetDynaClass

ResultSetDynaClass is not good enough in cases where it is likely that the ResultSet can get closed before the processing of the DynaBean is complete or in cases where the contents of the ResultSet are to be sent across application tiers. In this case, the ResultSet is bound to be invalid.

RowSetDynaClass provides an alternative where the contents of the ResultSet are copied into DynaBeans that exist in memory. Once this process is complete, whatever might happen to the ResultSet, you still have your DynaBeans to use. For example, if your application has a data access layer that is meant to query a database and return data in the form of data objects to the business logic layer, the RowSetDynaClass can be useful because you could now return DynaBeans that are independent of the ResultSet.

The only bit of code change from the ResultSetDynaTrial code that occurs is that you now close the ResultSet immediately after creating RowSetDynaClass and then get a list of rows over which you iterate. The new bit of code is as follows:

```
RowSetDynaClass rsDynaClass= new RowSetDynaClass(rs);
//Close ResultSet right away
rs.close();
List rows= rsDynaClass.getRows();
Iterator itr= rows.iterator();
```

RowSetDynaClass, however, will take up more resources because many new objects independent of those referenced by the ResultSet have to be created.

NOTE *In these examples, you deal with specific types of* DynaClass *such as* BasicDynaClass, ResultSetDynaClass, RowSetDynaClass, *and* WrapDynaClass; *however, you stay away from using references of specific types of* DynaBean *because you should not be using features beyond those provided by the basic* DynaBean *interface.*

WrapDynaClass

In all these examples, you have used the PropertyUtils class to set and get properties. However, all DynaBeans also provide get methods that can handle the same functionality as provided by the getSimpleProperty, getIndexedProperty, and getMappedProperty methods.

The PropertyUtils methods will work for all beans, DynaBeans or otherwise. So you can safely use the PropertyUtils methods for both kinds of beans. However, if you want to use all beans as DynaBeans and use the get and set methods provided in the DynaBean interface, you have to wrap the beans that are not DynaBeans. WrapDynaClass is meant to serve that purpose. You will now look at an example where you create instances of the Person and Computer classes you used in Listing 5-3 and wrap them into DynaBeans. Listing 5-6 displays the same property access capabilities you saw in the Listing 5-3 PropertyUtils example.

Listing 5-6. WrapDynaTrial *Class*

```
package com.commonsbook.chap5;
import org.apache.commons.beanutils.DynaBean;
import org.apache.commons.beanutils.WrapDynaBean;

import java.util.ArrayList;
import java.util.HashMap;

public class WrapDynaTrial {
    public static void main(String[] args) throws Exception {
        DynaBean personDyBean = new WrapDynaBean(new Person());
```

```
personDyBean.set("name", "Mr. X");
personDyBean.set("age", new Integer(30));
personDyBean.set("pastEmployers",
    new String[] { "Microsoft", "Sun", "IBM" });

//ArrayList of certifications
ArrayList cert = new ArrayList();
cert.add("SCJP");
cert.add("SCWCD");

//Set simple properties
personDyBean.set("certifications", cert);
personDyBean.set("phoneNumbers", new HashMap());
personDyBean.set("homeComputer", new Computer());
personDyBean.set("workComputer", new Computer());

//Set indexed properties
personDyBean.set("pastEmployers", 0, "BEA");
personDyBean.set("certifications", 1, "SCEA");

//Set mapped properties
personDyBean.set("phoneNumbers", "home", "111222333");
personDyBean.set("phoneNumbers", "office", "00000000");

//Set nested properties
DynaBean homeComp = new WrapDynaBean(personDyBean.get("homeComputer"));
homeComp.set("processor", "Intel P4");
homeComp.set("ramDetails", "512 MB");
homeComp.set("operatingSystem", "Win2K");

System.out.println("***Simple Property Access***");
System.out.println("\tSimpProp name= " + personDyBean.get("name"));
System.out.println("\tSimpProp age= " + personDyBean.get("age"));

System.out.println("***Mapped Property Access***");
System.out.println("\tMapProp phoneNumbers > home= " +
    personDyBean.get("phoneNumbers", "home"));
System.out.println("\tMapProp phoneNumbers > office= " +
    personDyBean.get("phoneNumbers", "office"));

System.out.println("***Indexed Property Access***");
System.out.println("\tIndProp pastEmployers[0] = " +
    personDyBean.get("pastEmployers", 0));
System.out.println("\tIndProp certifications[1] = " +
    personDyBean.get("certifications", 1));
```

```
        System.out.println("***Nested Property Access***");
        System.out.println("\tNestedProperty homeComputer.processor = " +
            new WrapDynaBean(personDyBean.get("homeComputer")).get("processor"));
        System.out.println("\tNestedProperty homeComputer.ramDetails = " +
            new WrapDynaBean(personDyBean.get("homeComputer")).get("ramDetails"));
        System.out.println("\tNestedProperty homeComputer.operatingSystem = " +
            new WrapDynaBean(personDyBean.get("homeComputer")).get(
                "operatingSystem"));
    }
}
```

The output upon executing the class WrapDynaTrial is as follows:

```
***Simple Property Access***
  SimpProp name= Mr. X
  SimpProp age= 30
***Mapped Property Access***
  MapProp phoneNumbers > home= 111222333
  MapProp phoneNumbers > office= 00000000
***Indexed Property Access***
  IndProp pastEmployers[0] = BEA
  IndProp certifications[1] = SCEA
***Nested Property Access***
  NestedProperty homeComputer.processor = Intel P4
  NestedProperty homeComputer.ramDetails = 512 MB
  NestedProperty homeComputer.operatingSystem = Win2K
```

In this example, you only use DynaBean references to access objects. Although working with simple, mapped, and indexed properties is simple enough, working with nested properties gets a little tricky because you have to keep wrapping the Computer class instances you use.

With WrapDynaClass, you now have the option of either sticking with the PropertyUtils class for all property access or wrapping beans into DynaBeans. I recommend using PropertyUtils because you can get started with it quickly, and you will probably commit fewer errors. You will now quickly look at another useful class in the BeanUtils component, the BeanComparator.

Using the BeanComparator Class

As the name suggests, the BeanComparator class compares beans. The BeanComparator class compares instances based on the value of a certain property in the beans. It essentially calls the getXxx method for the beans and, based on the values returned, completes the comparison. Listing 5-7 shows how you compare two instances of the Person class you created earlier in the chapter.

Listing 5-7. `BeanComparatorTrial`

```
package com.commonsbook.chap5;
import org.apache.commons.beanutils.BeanComparator;

public class BeanComparatorTrial {
    public static void main(String[] args) {
        Person p1 = new Person();
        p1.setAge(30);

        Person p2 = new Person();
        p2.setAge(20);

        BeanComparator bcomp = new BeanComparator("age");
        System.out.println("On comparing p1 with p2 >>>"+bcomp.compare(p1, p2));
    }
}
```

In this example, you create two instances of the Person class and set the age for both instances. You next create a BeanComparator instance and pass age as the parameter to the constructor. This creates a new BeanComparator that will compare based on the value of the property age. You next call the compare method and pass both instances of the Person class. The output upon execution is as follows:

```
On comparing p1 with p2 >>>1
```

Because the age for p1 is greater than p2, the output is 1. It would have been 0 if the two were equal and -1 if the age of p2 was greater than p1.

Summary

In this chapter, you used the BeanUtils component to handle routine tasks that take up a lot of time and effort. BeanUtils can streamline your code as well as reduce the number of classes you have to write.

The BeanUtils component is one of the top offerings of the Commons project and, considering its relevance to a wide gamut of Java projects, is one package you should consider adopting right away.

CHAPTER 6

Implementing Pooling

UNLIKE THE EARLIER CHAPTERS, this chapter is not dedicated to a particular component but instead deals with two components: Pool and Database Connection Pool (DBCP).

Pooling is an important concept and, if used wisely, can reduce resource consumption as well as boost your applications' performance. However, note that with newer application servers claiming to already use object pooling quite extensively, implementing pooling in your application might not always be required. Table 6-1 shows the details for the components covered in this chapter.

Table 6-1. Component Details

Name	Version	Package
Pool	1.0.1	`org.apache.commons.pool`
Database Connection Pool (DBCP)	1.0	`org.apache.commons.dbcp`

Why Use Pooling?

The ways of pooling resources might vary; however, the core idea is to minimize creation and destruction of objects and reuse objects as much as possible.

Although object pooling is a general concept concerned with maintaining a pool of all kinds of objects, database connection pooling is a more specialized concept concerned only with the pooling of database connections. Database connection pooling is quite an old practice, and the reason it is popular is that it is a lot less expensive to pool and reuse database connections than to keep creating and destroying them. The same idea applies to instance pooling; however, instance pooling emerged primarily after the dawn of Java 2 Enterprise Edition (J2EE) application servers. Many servers boast of providing complex algorithms and logic to pool instances.

So, if you are using a J2EE application server, I recommend you use a resource-monitoring tool such as OptimizeIt or Oracle JDeveloper's built-in resource monitoring tools to first check if implementing pooling separately is really required. I say this because most application servers provide for pooling objects and database connections, so having a separate pooling exercise might be quite unnecessary. If you think your server is not doing much and an unreasonable number of objects are being created, implementing pooling using the components discussed in this chapter is a smart choice.

Load testing an application is one area where the need for pooling becomes quite obvious. For example, while testing a Web site, the server and the Java Virtual Machine (JVM) can easily handle the occasional hit or two, and resource consumption will not be a problem. However, when these hits reach the thousands, if the application is not using resources wisely, then your application and the server can come to a grinding halt.

In this chapter, you will first look at the Pool component. The DBCP component uses the Pool component to implement database connection pooling, so understanding the DBCP component will be easier once you understand Pool. The home page for the pool component is at `http://jakata.apache.org/commons/pool/`, and the home page for DBCP is at `http://jakata.apache.org/commons/dbcp/`. The DBCP component depends on the Pool component, and the Pool component depends on the Commons Collections component.

Using the Pool Component

The Pool component consists of two packages: `org.apache.commons.pool` and `org.apache.commons.pool.impl`. The package `org.apache.commons.pool` provides interfaces and base implementations, and the `org.apache.commons.pool.impl` package provides implementations of a few types of object pooling that are possible.

The `ObjectPool` interface is what defines the methods that each pooling implementation has to provide. The interface is simple enough; the methods `borrowObject` and `returnObject` are the two you will use the most.

GenericObjectPool

You will now see an example where you use the provided `GenericObjectPool` implementation to pool objects of a class `Computer` that you will define. The `Computer` class has the following three properties and their corresponding public getter and setter methods:

```
private String processor;
private String operatingSystem;
private String location;
```

Before you pool instances of a certain class, you need to define a `Factory` class that will be used to create, destroy, activate, passivate, and validate instances of the class. The `PoolableObjectFactory` interface defines the methods to be used, and you have the option of directly implementing these methods or extending the base implementation `BasePoolableObjectFactory` that is provided. In this example, you will go with extending `BasePoolableObjectFactory` because this way you are forced to implement only the abstract `makeObject` method. `BasePoolableObjectFactory` provides dummy implementations for the other methods, and you have the option of overriding these.

The methods of `PoolableObjectFactory` are as follows:

- **makeObject**: This method is called whenever the need to create a new object instance for the pool arises. In this implementation, you instantiate the class whose instances are to be pooled, set any properties you want to be present in all instances, and then return the instance.

- **activateObject**: This method is invoked when you want to borrow an object from the pool. Just before the pool gives an object to the application code, this method is invoked; you can also set any properties at this stage.

- **passivateObject**: This method is invoked when the application code returns an object it borrowed earlier. You can insert code to free resources used by that instance.

- **destroyObject**: This is invoked to destroy an instance and is invoked when the pool is being closed or when validation for an instance fails.

- **validateObject**: This is a useful method to ensure that the pool always returns instances that are in a valid state.

You will create a new `Factory` class named `ComputerObjFactory` and implement the methods `makeObject` and `passivateObject`. Listing 6-1 shows the code for the Factory class.

Listing 6-1. `ComputerObjFactory`

```
package com.commonsbook.chap6;
import org.apache.commons.pool.BasePoolableObjectFactory;

public class ComputerObjFactory extends BasePoolableObjectFactory {
    static int i = 1;

    public Object makeObject() {
        System.out.println("\t [ComputerObjFactory] Created object " + i++);

        return new Computer();
    }
```

```
    public void passivateObject(Object obj) {
        if (obj != null) {
            System.out.println("\t [ComputerObjFactory] Passivating object");

            Computer c = (Computer) obj;
            c.setOperatingSystem(null);
            c.setProcessor(null);
            c.setLocation(null);
        }
    }
}
```

In the makeObject method, you simply return a new instance of the Computer class, and in the passivateObject method, you clear up all values for the instance that was returned to the pool. The instance continues in an idle state in the pool.

Now that you have the Factory class ready, you can move on to the code where you create and use GenericObjectPool. GenericObjectPool is an implementation of ObjectPool that is provided as part of the component. GenericObjectPool is a suitable pooling methodology for most cases, and although possible, you do not need to provide a pooling mechanism specific to your application. An important feature of GenericObjectPool is that it is highly configurable. Listing 6-2 shows an example where you create a new GenericObjectPool of Computer objects and use the various features provided.

Listing 6-2. GenericObjectPoolTrial

```
package com.commonsbook.chap6;
import org.apache.commons.pool.impl.GenericObjectPool;

public class GenericObjectPoolTrial {
    public static void main(String[] args) {
        GenericObjectPool pool = new GenericObjectPool(new ComputerObjFactory());
        System.out.println("1) NumActive:" + pool.getNumActive() +
            "\tNumIdle: " + pool.getNumIdle());

        try {
            //Borrow two objects from pool
            Computer compHome = (Computer) pool.borrowObject();
            Computer compWork = (Computer) pool.borrowObject();

            System.out.println("2) NumActive:" + pool.getNumActive() +
                "\tNumIdle: " + pool.getNumIdle());

            //Return one object to pool
            pool.returnObject(compHome);
```

```
            System.out.println("3) NumActive:" + pool.getNumActive() +
                "\tNumIdle: " + pool.getNumIdle());

            //Clears the pool of all pooled instances
            pool.clear();

            System.out.println("4) NumActive:" + pool.getNumActive() +
                "\tNumIdle: " + pool.getNumIdle());

            //Close the pool
            pool.close();
        } catch (Exception e) {
            e.printStackTrace();
        }
    }
}
```

This code does the following:

1. Creates a pool of Computer class instances using ComputerObjFactory

2. Borrows two instances of Computer from the pool

3. Returns one of two instances borrowed

4. Clears the pool

5. Closes the pool

The output you get upon executing this piece of code should reveal how instance pooling works in this case:

```
1) NumActive:0   NumIdle: 0
          [ComputerObjFactory] Created object 1
          [ComputerObjFactory] Created object 2
2) NumActive:2   NumIdle: 0
          [ComputerObjFactory] Passivating object
3) NumActive:1   NumIdle: 1
4) NumActive:1   NumIdle: 0
```

Line 1 shows that, as before, you borrow an instance from the pool, and the pool does not hold any objects. Therefore, you get an active object count of zero and an idle object count of zero. This is followed by calls to the ComputerObjFactory class, which creates the two instances you borrow from the pool. On passivating one of these instances, you are left with one object in an active state and one in an idle state. The call to the clear method gets rid of objects in the idle state.

If you had provided implementations in the ComputerObjFactory class to other methods in the PoolableObjectFactory, you could also have traced calls for object activation, destruction, and so on.

You also have the option of using the GenericObjectPoolFactory class to create the pool. The GenericObjectPoolFactory class provides many constructors that can enable creation of a customized pool. The pool creation code in that case would be as follows:

```
GenericObjectPoolFactory gObjPoolFactory=
    new GenericObjectPoolFactory(new ComputerObjFactory());
GenericObjectPool pool = (GenericObjectPool)gObjPoolFactory.createPool();
```

This piece of code would replace the first line in the main method that creates a new instance of GenericObjectPool. You can also configure the GenericObjectPool object that you created to suit your specific requirements. You can call setter methods for the class GenericObjectPool that can configure the maximum number of active instances, maximum number of idle instances, whether to test the instance before returning, and so on. Try the various settings, and choose the one that best suits your application when running in a production environment.

You will now move on to another ObjectPool implementation that is provided as part of the package, GenericKeyedObjectPool.

GenericKeyedObjectPool

GenericKeyedObjectPool is an implementation similar to GenericObjectPool with regard to how it functions. The only change is that the objects in the pool are now associated against a certain key. So a pool of instances can have some instances with the key X and the rest with the key Z. Unlike GenericObjectPoolFactory, where all objects in the pool were the same, with GenericKeyedObjectPool, objects have their keys. As a result, when you want to borrow an instance from the pool, you also specify the key value. Based on this key value, only an instance whose key matches the requested key can be returned.

GenericKeyedObjectPool can get you a pool of similar objects with minor variations that are the keys. You will now see an example where, unlike the earlier example where you pooled instances of the Computer class, you will pool instances associated against a particular key. The keys for the example are home and work. You will now have some instances in the pool that have the key value as home and some that have the key value as work. This does not mean there are any restrictions on the number or type of keys. You are free to use as many keys as you want.

You need to create the Factory class responsible for generating the instances. You will now extend the base class BaseKeyedPoolableObjectFactory and implement the methods makeObject and validateObject (see Listing 6-3). The method names stay the same as with GenericObjectPool; however, the signatures vary a little.

Listing 6-3. ComputerKeyedObjFactory

```
package com.commonsbook.chap6;
import org.apache.commons.pool.BaseKeyedPoolableObjectFactory;

public class ComputerKeyedObjFactory extends BaseKeyedPoolableObjectFactory {
    static int i = 0;

    public Object makeObject(Object key) {
        System.out.println("\t [ComputerKeyedObjFactory] Created object " +
            ++i);

        return new Computer((String) key);
    }

    public boolean validateObject(Object key, Object obj) {
        System.out.println("\tValidating Object " + i);

        if ((obj != null) && (key != null)) {
            return true;
        } else {
            return false;
        }
    }
}
```

In the validateObject method you simply check if the arguments are not null. However, you could easily have had more complex checks. Also, while creating the objects of the class Computer, you use the key provided and create the Computer instance accordingly by passing the key as a parameter to the constructor of the Computer class.

Next, you write code to create and use the pool like in the GenericObjectPool example you saw earlier. In Listing 6-4, however, you have to print the state of the pool with reference to the two keys that you are using, home and work.

Listing 6-4. GenericKeyedObjectPoolTrial

```java
package com.commonsbook.chap6;
import org.apache.commons.pool.impl.GenericKeyedObjectPool;

public class GenericKeyedObjectPoolTrial {
    public static void main(String[] args) {
        GenericKeyedObjectPool keyPool =
                new GenericKeyedObjectPool(new ComputerKeyedObjFactory());

        //Validate objects being borrowed
        keyPool.setTestOnBorrow(true);

        System.out.println("1 home)NumActive:" + keyPool.getNumActive("home") +
            "\tNumIdle: " + keyPool.getNumIdle("home"));
        System.out.println("1 work)NumActive:" + keyPool.getNumActive("work") +
            "\tNumIdle: " + keyPool.getNumIdle("work"));

        try {
            //Borrow two objects from pool. Validate before returning
            Computer keyCompHome = (Computer) keyPool.borrowObject("home");
            Computer keyCompWork = (Computer) keyPool.borrowObject("work");

            System.out.println("2 home)NumActive:" +
                keyPool.getNumActive("home") + "\tNumIdle: " +
                keyPool.getNumIdle("home"));
            System.out.println("2 work)NumActive:" +
                keyPool.getNumActive("work") + "\tNumIdle: " +
                keyPool.getNumIdle("work"));

            //Return one object to pool
            keyPool.returnObject(keyCompHome.getLocation(), keyCompHome);

            System.out.println("3 home)NumActive:" +
                keyPool.getNumActive("home") + "\tNumIdle: " +
                keyPool.getNumIdle("home"));
            System.out.println("3 work)NumActive:" +
                keyPool.getNumActive("work") + "\tNumIdle: " +
                keyPool.getNumIdle("work"));

            //Clears the pool of all pooled instances
            keyPool.clear();
```

```
            System.out.println("4 home)NumActive:" +
                keyPool.getNumActive("home") + "\tNumIdle: " +
                keyPool.getNumIdle("home"));
            System.out.println("4 work)NumActive:" +
                keyPool.getNumActive("work") + "\tNumIdle: " +
                keyPool.getNumIdle("work"));

            //Close the pool
            keyPool.close();
        } catch (Exception e) {
            e.printStackTrace();
        }
    }
}
```

I will not go through how the entire example works because it is similar to the GenericObjectPool example earlier. The thing that changes is that you now use the setTestOnBorrow method to explicitly say you want to validate objects before the pool provides them to the client for use. Because this value is false by default, only if you set it to true will the validateObject method in the ComputerKeyedObjFactory class be called.

Also note that the code almost behaves like you have independent pools working for you. This is a big advantage of using GenericKeyedObjectPool. So instead of creating many pools in the code, if you make your pooling key-based, you can even decide at runtime how many and what type of keyed pools you require. The output is as follows:

```
1 home)NumActive:0       NumIdle: 0
1 work)NumActive:0       NumIdle: 0
          [ComputerKeyedObjFactory] Created object 1
        Validating Object 1
          [ComputerKeyedObjFactory] Created object 2
        Validating Object 2
2 home)NumActive:1       NumIdle: 0
2 work)NumActive:1       NumIdle: 0
3 home)NumActive:0       NumIdle: 1
3 work)NumActive:1       NumIdle: 0
4 home)NumActive:0       NumIdle: 0
4 work)NumActive:1       NumIdle: 0
```

Pool Implementations

Apart from the two pool implementations discussed, the other implementations provided in the package are as follows:

- **StackObjectPool**: This is an ObjectPool that uses java.util.Stack to maintain the pool so the pool works in a Last In First Out (LIFO) fashion.

- **StackKeyedObjectPool**: This is a KeyedObjectPool that also uses java.util.Stack to maintain the pool and support key-based pooling of instances.

- **SoftReferenceObjectPool**: This is a java.lang.ref.SoftReference based implementation of ObjectPool. This pool works in a LIFO fashion, and each object is wrapped in a java.lang.ref.SoftReference, allowing the garbage collector to remove idle instances from the pool if required.

Because all are implementations of the ObjectPool or KeyedObjectPool interface, the methods stay the same and the usage code also does not change too much.

Now that you have seen an overview of pooling and some of the implementations that you can use, you will learn about pooling database connections.

Understanding Database Connection Pooling

Whenever any performance-related issues crop up, invariably the first finger points toward the database. Most Java developers are quite convinced that their code is efficient and the database access is what is causing the slowdown.

Although that is frequently true, there are always means by which you can use fewer resources and make database access work a lot faster. Optimizing your SQL queries is what tops the list, but not far behind is the idea of pooling database connections. Obtaining connections is an expensive task, and so once you have invested in a connection, you might as well make better use of it than throwing it away after every use. Locating the database, establishing communication with it, and exchanging some information is what is involved in getting a new database connection. Going through this entire routine every time can be quite time consuming.

A database connection pool is where you keep your expensive connections, use them when required, and return them to the pool. The features you can expect from a database connection pool are as follows:

- Should be scalable and have the ability to generate new connections as and when required.

- Should not hog resources by maintaining too many connections in the pool. It should release connections when usage is low.

- Pooling mechanism should be configurable, fast, and efficient.

- Should not be limited to a certain database. In the Java context, a Java Database Connection (JDBC) driver should be the only requirement.

The DBCP component does provide these features and because it uses the Pool component discussed earlier, the features of that component also exist in DBCP.

On my first encounter with DBCP, I cannot say I found it very simple or easy to use. DBCP can appear quite complex, especially if you encounter it even before you understand how the pooling component works.

So instead of going into the theory and classes of DBCP, you will look at more DBCP examples because usage is what matters. There are simple ways of using DBCP, and once you get the hang of it, you could easily reuse the code from these examples.

TIP   *The DBCP download comes with examples of how to use DBCP in various ways.*

For the database connection pooling examples I will use a database named test running on MySQL server. You can download the MySQL server and the JDBC driver for it from http://www.mysql.com/. The host name is localhost, and the port is 3306. On this database, create a table named Student. The table creation query is as follows:

```
CREATE TABLE 'student' (
  'StudId' int(10) NOT NULL default '0',
  'Name' varchar(100) NOT NULL default ''
);
```

Alternatives

You have three ways of getting DBCP to generate a database connection pool. Two ways involve some coding, and the third achieves a similar end but by using an XML-based configuration file that conveys all the required configuration information.

NOTE   *The DBCP documentation says that there are two ways of generating a pool. This is correct, but I maintain that three ways exist because, unlike the documentation, I treat the XML file–based approach separately.*

The three ways are as follows:

- Using an XML file to define pool settings

- Creating an instance of `PoolingDriver`

- Creating an instance of `PoolingDataSource`

An important aspect of all three ways is using the `PoolableConnectionFactory` class. In the case of the first two, you write the code to create an instance of `PoolableConnectionFactory`; in the third case, you use the XML file to define all that is required to create an instance of `PoolableConnectionFactory`.

I think it is easiest to understand DBCP with reference to creating an instance of `PoolableConnectionFactory`. The `PoolableConnectionFactory` instance has to be created in all three ways, and it is responsible for returning the actual pooled connections.

You will begin with the way I think is the best and the simplest of the lot. Using this methodology, your code looks just like JDBC code looks otherwise. All the pooling and configuration details are picked up from an XML file.

JOCL-Based Pooling

Java Object Configuration Language (JOCL) provides for the construction of Java objects from XML. The documentation and DBCP member opinions on the Commons mailing lists seem to convey that DBCP will later move to using Commons Digester instead of JOCL. However, as of version 1.0, JOCL is used. All the JOCL classes are part of the component download, so no separate JOCL download is required. However, you will need an XML parser such as Xerces (http://xml.apache.org/) that supports Simple API for XML (SAX) 2. You also have to define the system property `org.xml.sax.driver`. The value will be `org.apache.xerces.parsers.SAXParser` if you are using Xerces. You can use the Java option -D to specify this property as follows:

```
-Dorg.xml.sax.driver=org.apache.xerces.parsers.SAXParser
```

With JOCL, what you do is just create an instance of a class based on the data provided in the form of XML. Because there are no separate classes in DBCP that have the logic for JOCL-based creation, you use the `PoolableConnectionFactory` for creation of the connections in all the different ways of DBCP pooling. With the JOCL way as well, you use this same class. However, you call the constructor of the class based on data provided in XML.

TIP *Think of the XML file in terms of providing details for calling the constructor of the* PoolableConnectionFactory *class. That is all the file does.*

Listing 6-5 shows, as a comment, the PoolableConnectionFactory constructor that you will be invoking using the data in the XML file jocltest.jocl. Note that the directory holding the file needs to be present in the CLASSPATH for the file to be located and used.

Listing 6-5. jocltest.jocl

```
<!--
    PoolableConnectionFactory(ConnectionFactory connFactory
    ,org.apache.commons.pool.ObjectPool pool
    ,org.apache.commons.pool.KeyedObjectPoolFactory stmtPoolFactory
    ,java.lang.String validationQuery
    ,boolean defaultReadOnly
    ,boolean defaultAutoCommit)
-->
<object class="org.apache.commons.dbcp.PoolableConnectionFactory"
xmlns="http://apache.org/xml/xmlns/jakarta/commons/jocl">

    <!--
        DriverManagerConnectionFactory(java.lang.String connectUri
        , java.lang.String uname
        , java.lang.String passwd)
    -->
    <object class="org.apache.commons.dbcp.DriverManagerConnectionFactory">
        <!--Connect URI-->
        <string value="jdbc:mysql://127.0.0.1:3306/test"/>

        <!--User Name-->
        <string null="true"/>

        <!--Password-->
        <string null="true"/>
    </object>

    <!--
        GenericObjectPool(PoolableObjectFactory factory
        , int maxActive)
    -->
```

```
<object class="org.apache.commons.pool.impl.GenericObjectPool">
    <!-- null-->
    <object class="org.apache.commons.pool.PoolableObjectFactory" null="true"/>

    <!-- Maximum Active in Pool -->
    <int value="20"/>
</object>

<!-- Required for pooling Staetements against a particular connection-->
<object class="org.apache.commons.pool.KeyedObjectPoolFactory" null="true"/>

<!--    By default no validation is performed.
If required, specify appropriate query   -->
<string null="true"/>

<!-- Read Only-->
<boolean value="false"/>

<!-- Auto Commit -->
<boolean value="true"/>
</object>
```

You should notice that in the comments in the XML file, I have stated the Java constructors to which you are trying to map. Because the contents of the XML are meant to create a PoolableConnectionFactory, that is the first constructor stated.

 TIP *Have a look at the Application Programming Interface (API) specifications for the classes being used to find more details about the various parameters being passed to the* PoolableConnectionFactory *constructor.*

This XML provides all the details to create a GenericObjectPool of database connections to the MySQL database named test I am running locally at 127.0.0.1, port 3306. Change these details for your specific scenario. Most of the classes being used here provide more than one constructor, so you also have the option to specify more details to create a customized instance.

What the XML does is as follows:

1. Create a `DriverManagerConnectionFactory` to the specified Uniform Resource Indicator (URI). The username and password are null for this particular case.

2. Create a `GenericObjectPool` that can have 20 maximum active instances. You have the choice of using other implementations provided by the Pool component, such as `StackObjectPool` or `SoftReferencePool`.

3. You specify a `null` value for `KeyedObjectPoolFactory`. These keyed pools can be used to store `PreparedStatements` against particular connections.

4. You specify no query to validate instances before the pool returns them.

5. The pool is meant only for read-only operations, and the autocommit feature is enabled.

Next you need to write the code that will use the connection pool. An important aspect of using the JOCL way is that the Java code stays exactly as it would if you were using normal JDBC. Apart from making things simpler for developers, it also makes it possible to disable connection pooling easily.

Listing 6-6 shows the Java code to fetch the records in the `Student` table.

Listing 6-6. `JOCLPoolingTrial`

```
package com.commonsbook.chap6;
import java.sql.Connection;
import java.sql.DriverManager;
import java.sql.ResultSet;
import java.sql.Statement;

public class JOCLPoolingTrial {
    public static void main(String[] args) {
        Connection conn = null;
        Statement stmt = null;
        ResultSet rset = null;

        try {
            //jocltest is stated in the connection URI
            String uri = "jdbc:apache:commons:dbcp:/jocltest";

            //The query to be executed
            String query = "SELECT StudId, Name FROM student";
```

```
                    //MySQL JDBC driver
                    Class.forName("com.mysql.jdbc.Driver");
                    Class.forName("org.apache.commons.dbcp.PoolingDriver");

                    conn = DriverManager.getConnection(uri);
                    stmt = conn.createStatement();
                    rset = stmt.executeQuery(query);

                    while (rset.next()) {
                        System.out.println(rset.getString(1) + "\t" +
                            rset.getString(2));
                    }
            } catch (Exception e) {
                e.printStackTrace();
            } finally {
                try {
                    if (rset != null) {
                        rset.close();
                    }

                    if (stmt != null) {
                        stmt.close();
                    }

                    if (conn != null) {
                        conn.close();
                    }
                } catch (Exception e) {
                    e.printStackTrace();
                }
            }
        }
    }
}
```

In this piece of code, the only code that is not standard JDBC is where you define the URI and load two drivers. The connection URI does not define the actual location of the database but is a DBCP-specific URI. Also note :/jocltest, which is stated in the URI. Based on this, the corresponding file jocltest.jocl is looked up. The file has to be in the CLASSPATH for it to be found and used.

Also, Class.forName loads the two driver classes. You have to load both—the JDBC driver for the database you are using as well as the DBCP PoolingDriver. That is it—you are now using a database connection pool! The program output contains all the records in the Student table, which in the case of the table contents I had, are as follows:

1	One
2	Two
3	Three

I recommend you use the JOCL method of database connection pooling because it keeps the code free of any DBCP-specific code. Also, thanks to the XML file, the pool stays easily configurable. You will next look at how connection pooling is possible by creating an instance of PoolingDriver or PoolingDataSource.

PoolingDriver and PoolingDataSource

I will now discuss the other ways of obtaining a database connection pool using DBCP. Because there is a lot of overlap between the PoolingDriver and the Pooling DataSource ways, I will use a combined example to illustrate the similarities and differences between the two (see Listing 6-7).

This example also uses the same database and table used for the JOCL example earlier. Because these two ways are completely code based and do not involve using any configuration file, you have to write a little more code than in the earlier case. Also, the code moves away from basic JDBC code to more DBCP-specific code.

Listing 6-7. PoolingDriverDataSourceTrial

```java
package com.commonsbook.chap6;
import java.sql.*;

import javax.sql.*;

import org.apache.commons.dbcp.*;
import org.apache.commons.pool.*;
import org.apache.commons.pool.impl.*;

public class PoolingDriverDataSourceTrial {
    public static void main(String[] args) {
        Connection connUsingDriver = null;
        Connection connUsingDataSource = null;
        Statement stmt = null;
        ResultSet rset = null;

        try {
            //Load MySQL Driver
            Class.forName("com.mysql.jdbc.Driver");
```

```
            //URI for test database
            String uri = "jdbc:mysql://127.0.0.1:3306/test";

            //PoolingDriver Section
            registerPoolingDriver(uri);
            connUsingDriver = DriverManager.getConnection(
                    "jdbc:apache:commons:dbcp:test");
            System.out.println("[PoolingDriver] DB Name = " +
                connUsingDriver.getMetaData().getDatabaseProductName());

            //PoolingDataSource Section
            DataSource dataSrc = getPoolingDataSource(uri);
            connUsingDataSource = dataSrc.getConnection();
            System.out.println("[PoolingDataSource] DB Name = " +
                connUsingDataSource.getMetaData().getDatabaseProductName());
        } catch (Exception e) {
            e.printStackTrace();
        } finally {
            try {
                if (rset != null) {
                    rset.close();
                }

                if (stmt != null) {
                    stmt.close();
                }

                if (connUsingDriver != null) {
                    connUsingDriver.close();
                }

                if (connUsingDataSource != null) {
                    connUsingDataSource.close();
                }
            } catch (Exception e) {
                e.printStackTrace();
            }
        }
    }

    /**Get a PoolingDataSource      */
    private static DataSource getPoolingDataSource(String uri)
        throws Exception {
        ObjectPool connPool = getConnPool(uri);
        DataSource dataSrc = new PoolingDataSource(connPool);
```

```
        return dataSrc;
    }


    /**Register a PoolingDriver        */
    private static void registerPoolingDriver(String uri)
        throws Exception {
        ObjectPool connPool = getConnPool(uri);
        PoolingDriver driver = new PoolingDriver();
        driver.registerPool("test", connPool);
    }


    /**Get Connection Pool        */
    private static ObjectPool getConnPool(String uri) throws Exception {
        ObjectPool connPool = new GenericObjectPool(null);
        ConnectionFactory connFactory = new DriverManagerConnectionFactory(uri,
                null);
        PoolableConnectionFactory poolableConnFactory =
                new PoolableConnectionFactory(connFactory,
                connPool, null, null, false, true);

        return connPool;
    }
}
```

In this piece of code you first get a connection using the PoolingDriver way and then get a connection using PoolingDataSource. The steps involved in the case of PoolingDriver are as follows:

1. Get the connection pool using the method getConnPool.

2. Create a new PoolingDriver.

3. Register the connection pool with PoolingDriver under a certain name. In this case, the name is test.

4. Get a connection from the DriverManager using the pool name test.

In the case of PoolingDataSource, the steps are as follows:

1. Get the connection pool using the method getConnPool.

2. Create a new PoolingDriver using the connection pool.

3. Get a connection from the data source.

You should note that because the method `getConnPool` that creates the connection pool is being shared in both forms, a lot of the code gets reused. Once you have the connection pool, things get pretty simple. In the case of `PoolingDriver`, you register the pool using this:

```
PoolingDriver driver = new PoolingDriver();
driver.registerPool("test",connPool);
```

Next, you get the pool from the `DriverManager` using these lines of code:

```
connUsingDriver = DriverManager.getConnection("jdbc:apache:commons:dbcp:test");
```

Once you have the connection, you go back to the normal JDBC usage of connections. In the case of `PoolingDataSource`, again you get the connection pool using the `getConnPool` method. You then create the data source using the following line of code:

```
DataSource dataSrc = new PoolingDataSource(connPool);
```

From this data source, you then get a connection using the following line of code and again move to normal JDBC usage:

```
connUsingDataSource = dataSrc.getConnection();
```

As you saw in this example, it takes just a few lines of code to create and use a database connection pool. Although I recommend you use the XML file approach, even the code-based approaches are not too much trouble.

Integrating DBCP with Struts

You can integrate the DBCP component quite easily with the Struts framework (http://jakarta.apache.org/struts/). All you need to do is to configure a new data source in the `struts-config.xml` file and then get the data source using the `getDataSource` method in your `Action` class. Listing 6-8 shows the data source configuration in the `struts-config.xml` file.

Listing 6-8. New Data Source in `struts-config.xml`

```
<data-sources>
    <data-source type="org.apache.commons.dbcp.BasicDataSource"
                 key="testDS">
        <set-property property="driverClassName"
```

```
                         value="com.mysql.jdbc.Driver"/>
        <set-property property="url"
                       value="jdbc:mysql://127.0.0.1:3306/test"/>
        <set-property property="username"
                       value="test"/>
        <set-property property="password"
                       value="test"/>
        <set-property property="maxActive"
                       value="10"/>
        <set-property property="maxWait"
                       value="5000"/>
        <set-property property="defaultAutoCommit"
                       value="false"/>
        <set-property property="defaultReadOnly"
                       value="false"/>
        <set-property property="minIdle"
                       value="2"/>
        <set-property property="autoCommit"
                       value="false"/>
    </data-source>
</data-sources>
```

Here you configure a data source whose key is testDS. You also define various configuration properties for the data source. The Action class code to get this data source is as follows:

```
javax.sql.DataSource datasource= getDataSource(request, "testDS");
```

Once you have the data source, you can easily get a database connection from it using the getConnection provided.

Summary

In this chapter, you learned about the Pool component and the DBCP component. You next saw some examples of how you can use the various kinds of object pooling and how DBCP builds on object pooling to provide database connection pooling.

With regard to where you should use these components to introduce pooling, I suggest that if you have invested in an advanced J2EE application server such as WebSphere, WebLogic, JBoss, and so on, you do not take the additional trouble to implement these components. Instead, make good use of similar features provided by the application server. If your application server is not doing any object and database connection pooling for you, the components discussed in the chapter are just what you need.

#### CHAPTER 7

Using the Digester Component

THE EMERGENCE OF Extensible Markup Language (XML) has led to a complete transformation of the application development world. All development seems to revolve around XML these days. In fact, it is difficult to find any new development that does not directly or indirectly rely on XML. For instance, Web services are unimaginable without XML, and with the usage of Web services projected to boom over the next few years, there is no escaping XML.

In this chapter, you will look at the Digester component, which can simplify using XML. Table 7-1 shows the component details.

Table 7-1. Component Details

Name	Version	Package
Digester	1.5	`org.apache.commons.digester`

Introducing Digester

One problem that has plagued XML development is the complexity of parsing and using XML. Everybody knows the advantages of using XML, but I doubt many people are able to write a piece of code that parses an XML file and picks up the value of a certain XML tag. Writing a piece of Java code to parse a piece of XML directly using the two core Application Programming Interfaces (APIs)—the Document Object Model (DOM) and Simple API for XML (SAX)—is anything but simple. APIs such as JDOM are relatively simple, but considering how often you have to encounter and tackle XML, Digester provides an easier option. You can be parsing and using XML in your Java code in less than the time it will take you to read this chapter. (No, I will not eat my hat if you do not manage to accomplish the task.)

To quickly get up and running with Digester, you will see an example first. Do not worry about the syntax because you will look at that in detail later in this chapter. The scenario for this example is that you are presented with an XML file containing the details of all the students attending the various courses at your training institute. What you are expected to do is to pick up all the details present in the XML file, and for each student detail, populate an instance of a class Student, which you create. You will then store all the Student instances created in an instance of the java.util.Vector class for further processing.

You first need to create a Student class that will hold the details of a student (see Listing 7-1).

Listing 7-1. Student *Class*

```
package com.commonsbook.chap7;

public class Student {
    private String name;
    private String course;

    public Student() {
    }

    public String getName() {
        return name;
    }

    public void setName(String newName) {
        name = newName;
    }

    public String getCourse() {
        return course;
    }

    public void setCourse(String newCourse) {
        course = newCourse;
    }
    public String toString() {
        return("Name="+this.name + " & Course=" +  this.course);
    }
}
```

Apart from the overridden toString method, there is nothing special about this class. It has just two properties with getter and setter methods for each. You want to create instances of this class based on the data you retrieve from an XML file.

Listing 7-2 shows the XML file contents. The number of student tags is not relevant; you could very well introduce more students if you like.

Listing 7-2. `students.xml`

```xml
<?xml version="1.0"?>
<students>
        <student>
                <name>Java Boy</name>
                <course>JSP</course>
        </student>
        <student>
                <name>Java Girl</name>
                <course>EJB</course>
        </student>
</students>
```

 NOTE *In Listings 7-1 and 7-2 you can see that the names of the tags and properties match exactly. So, for a tag* course, *you have a property named* course *in the* Student *class. However, you can have different tag names and property names. No mapping of the XML and the Java class is required; you could very well store the value of a tag* ABC *into a property* XYZ. *The matching names merely keep things simple.*

The Java class DigestStudents, shown in Listing 7-3, will pick up the contents of the various XML tags and create a Vector class instance that can hold many instances of the class Student.

Listing 7-3. DigestStudents

```java
package com.commonsbook.chap7;

import java.util.Vector;
import org.apache.commons.digester.Digester;

public class DigestStudents {
    Vector students;

    public DigestStudents() {
        students= new Vector();
    }

    public static void main(String[] args) {
        DigestStudents digestStudents = new DigestStudents();
```

```
            digestStudents.digest();
    }

    private void digest() {
        try {
            Digester digester = new Digester();
            //Push the current object onto the stack
            digester.push(this);

            //Creates a new instance of the Student class
            digester.addObjectCreate( "students/student", Student.class );

            //Uses setName method of the Student instance
            //Uses tag name as the property name
            digester.addBeanPropertySetter( "students/student/name");

            //Uses setCourse method of the Student instance
            //Explicitly specify property name as 'course'
            digester.addBeanPropertySetter( "students/student/course", "course" );

            //Move to next student
            digester.addSetNext( "students/student", "addStudent" );

            DigestStudents ds = (DigestStudents) digester.parse(this.getClass()
                            .getClassLoader()
                            .getResourceAsStream("students.xml"));

            //Print the contents of the Vector
            System.out.println("Students Vector "+ds.students);
        } catch (Exception ex) {
            ex.printStackTrace();
        }
    }

    public void addStudent( Student stud ) {
        //Add a new Student instance to the Vector
        students.add( stud );
    }
}
```

In very few lines of code you have managed to create the Vector of Student instances. The output of the program is as follows, displaying the tag values in the file students.xml:

```
Students Vector [Name=Java Boy Course=JSP, Name=Java Girl Course=EJB]
```

Pretty cool, eh? I would have loved to write the corresponding DOM and SAX code to compare and illustrate the advantage of using the Digester component, but writing DOM and SAX code is something I forgot a long time ago and am not very keen on learning again. So you will just continue with the Digester experiments. Specifically, you will next look at some Digester fundamentals and learn how the example in Listing 7-3 works.

Understanding Digester Concepts

The Digester component has its origins in the Struts framework project. It began its life as a tool to quickly parse the `struts-config.xml` file without having to directly interact with SAX. Because the Digester functionality can be useful to all kinds of applications, it was later moved to the Commons project.

The Digester is not an XML parser but just a high-level interface that uses SAX underneath to accomplish the actual XML parsing. So a requirement for Digester is the presence of an XML parser conforming to Java API for XML Processing (JAXP) version 1.1 or later. The Digester also depends on the following Commons components:

- The BeanUtils component

- The Collections component

- The Logging component

Because Digester uses SAX to do the parsing, XML processing with Digester happens in an event-driven manner. An event-driven manner is when events are triggered while the document is being parsed; what you need to do is provide handlers for these events. That is the way SAX works. SAX is all about events being fired when a certain occurrence is found. SAX events are fired on occurrences such as starting tags, ending tags, and so on. DOM works a little differently: Object models are created in memory and parsed. However, when using the Digester, you do not need to understand how SAX or DOM works, and you do not need to do any SAX-specific tasks in your code. Just stick to Digester's rules, and you should soon be parsing XML documents with ease.

Digester uses a stack to store or retrieve objects as the XML file is being parsed. If you are not familiar with what a stack is, just think of it as a box in which you keep putting items and can remove them only on the basis of Last In First Out (LIFO). Java provides a stack implementation with `java.util.Stack`.

Based on the rules defined and the XML encountered, the Digester component pushes objects on the stack. Upon encountering the start of a tag, the associated object is pushed onto the stack, and it is popped only after all the nested contents of that tag are processed. So, in Listing 7-3 upon the student tag being encountered, an instance of Student class will be pushed onto the stack and will be popped once the processing of its child tags name and course is complete.

Using Matching Patterns

The big advantage of using the Digester component instead of other APIs is the presence of element matching patterns. Unlike other APIs where you have to worry about parent/child relationships among tags, what is important with Digester is the matching pattern specified. For example, in Listing 7-3, you used the matching patterns students/student, students/student/name, and students/student/course. This is an easy and developer-friendly usage to precisely convey the tag to which you want to refer. If you have to map the tags in Listing 7-2 to the corresponding matching pattern, the mapping will be as shown in Table 7-2.

Table 7-2. Tag Pattern Mapping

Tag	Pattern
<students>	students
<student>	students/student
<name>	students/student/name
<course>	students/student/course

You can also use the wildcard * if you want to have a more generalized matching. So the pattern */name would have matched all name tags within the document.

Using Rules

With element matching patterns you convey the exact location of the tag in the XML structure. However, to tell the Digester component what needs to be done upon finding that tag, you need to define processing rules. These rules fire when the matching pattern is found. All rules are expected to extend the abstract class org.apache.commons.digester.Rule and define specific actions that need to be taken when a certain element occurs.

You can define your own rules to handle application-specific cases. The Digester component comes with a set of rule implementations that extend the Rule class; you can find them in the package org.apache.commons.digester. As you move along, you will see some of these rules in the examples. In Listing 7-3 you used ObjectCreateRule to create an instance of the Student class, and you used BeanPropertySetterRule to set the properties of the class.

Before getting into a more complex XML example than the one you saw in Listing 7-2, you will look at the steps you need to perform for Digester to successfully retrieve data from XML:

1. You need to create a new instance of
    `org.apache.commons.digester.Digester` and configure it using the various
    `setXxx` methods provided by the class. Among other properties, you can
    define whether the XML should be validated, define the logger to be
    used, and define the `Rules` implementation object.

2. You push any initial objects on the object stack using the Digester's `push`
    method before you define the patterns and the rules to be used. In
    Listing 7-3, you pushed the current object on the stack using the keyword
    `this`. The reason you need to push this initial object is because Digester
    keeps pushing and popping objects from the stack as it encounters tags.
    So the first object is created and pushed onto the stack upon encounter-
    ing the first tag, and this object is popped off the stack when the last tag
    is processed. Because you need to hold a reference to the object for the
    first tag, the initial object you push before you parse the XML serves the
    purpose and retains a reference to that object.

3. Register element matching patterns and the rules you want to be fired
    for each case. In Listing 7-3 you register three patterns and two rules
    that you want to be fired.

4. Finally, you parse the XML file using the `parse` method of the Digester
    instance you created.

 NOTE *The order in which you do things is important for Digester.*
You cannot randomly move around statements before the call to
the parse *method. For example, in Listing 7-3, you cannot move the*
call to addObjectCreate *to after the call to* addSetNext.

You will now look at a more complex XML example and try to process it
using Digester. You will also see how you can move the specifying of Digester
patterns and rules from code to a configuration XML file.

Following XML Rules

In Listing 7-3, most of the code is dedicated to configuring the Digester instance.
Hardly any of the code can be termed as *action-oriented code*. The most common
usage of Digester is to process XML-based configuration files. The reason why these

configuration files are used is to keep code free of configuration information and make changes possible without having to change the code and recompile it. It would be unfair if you placed Digester configuration information within Java code. Even this bit has to move to a configuration XML file.

The package org.apache.commons.digester.xmlrules deals with this issue, and the DigesterLoader class that is present in this package makes it possible to create a Digester instance using just the information in an XML file.

In the following example, you will first look at Java code that will accomplish the task along somewhat similar lines as the example in Listing 7-3 and then move to an XML-based configuration file for the same example.

Listing 7-4 shows the XML file from which you want to fetch information. The XML stores information about an academy, its students, and its teachers. The Digester code picks up these details and makes them manageable within Java code.

Listing 7-4. academy.xml

```xml
<?xml version="1.0"?>
<academy name="JAcademy" >
        <student name="JavaBoy" division="A">
                <course>
                     <id>C1</id>
                     <name>JSP</name>
                </course>
                <course>
                     <id>C2</id>
                     <name>Servlets</name>
                </course>
        </student>
        <student name="JavaGirl" division="B">
                <course>
                     <id>C3</id>
                     <name>EJB</name>
                </course>
        </student>

        <teacher name="JavaGuru">
                <certification>SCJP</certification>
                <certification>SCWCD</certification>
        </teacher>
        <teacher name="JavaMaster">
                <certification>OCP</certification>
                <certification>SCJP</certification>
                <certification>SCEA</certification>
        </teacher>
</academy>
```

> **NOTE** *With Listing 7-4 I have tried to address the many scenarios you might encounter when parsing XML files. Reusing the code from this example can get you started in no time.*

Because you have to hold the XML data in Java objects, you need to decide which classes you have to create. Instances of these classes will hold the data for you. Looking at this example, you should see four classes that together can do a good job of holding the data in a properly structured format. These classes are Academy, Student, Course, and Teacher. You could very well create more classes, such as Certification. The most important thing is that you cannot have these as just separate classes; you also need to maintain the relationships among them as depicted in the XML file. So, you will first put down the Java classes. Instances of the Java classes will hold the data for you.

An instance of the Course class is meant to store just the name and the ID of the course. The Course instance will not be maintaining its relation to the Student; this will be done by the Student instance. Listing 7-5 shows the Course class; it has two properties and the corresponding get and set methods. Note that the package name for classes used in this example is com.commonsbook.chap7.academy.

Listing 7-5. Course *Class*

```
package com.commonsbook.chap7.academy;
import org.apache.commons.beanutils.PropertyUtils;

import java.util.Vector;

public class Course {
    private String id;
    private String name;

    public Course() {
    }

    public String getId() {
        return id;
    }

    public void setId(String newId) {
        id = newId;
    }
```

```
        public String getName() {
            return name;
        }

        public void setName(String newName) {
            name = newName;
        }

        public String toString() {
            StringBuffer buf = new StringBuffer(60);
            buf.append("\n\tCourseId>>> " + this.getId() + "\t");
            buf.append("CourseName>>> " + this.getName());

            return buf.toString();
        }
    }
```

Next you will define the Student class that not only has to hold information about the student but also about the courses the student attends. As shown in Listing 7-6, the student details are stored using properties, and the courses will be stored as a Vector of Course instances.

Listing 7-6. Student *Class*

```
package com.commonsbook.chap7.academy;
import java.util.Vector;

public class Student {
    private Vector courses;
    private String name;
    private String division;

    public Student() {
        courses = new Vector();
    }

    public void addCourse(Course course) {
        courses.addElement(course);
    }

    public String getName() {
        return name;
    }
```

```
    public void setName(String newName) {
        name = newName;
    }

    public String getDivision() {
        return division;
    }

    public void setDivision(String newDivision) {
        division = newDivision;
    }

    public void setCourses(Vector courses) {
        this.courses = courses;
    }

    public Vector getCourses() {
        return courses;
    }

    public String toString() {
        StringBuffer buf = new StringBuffer(60);

        buf.append("\nStudent name>> " + this.getName());

        Vector courses = this.getCourses();

        //Iterate through vector. Append content to StringBuffer.
        for (int i = 0; i < courses.size(); i++) {
            buf.append(courses.get(i));
        }

        return buf.toString();
    }
}
```

Listing 7-4 shows that, for a teacher, you are expected to store the name and the list of certifications held by the teacher. The Teacher class, shown in Listing 7-7, does this by using a String property for the name and a Vector holding String instances for the certifications list.

Listing 7-7. Teacher *Class*

```
package com.commonsbook.chap7.academy;
import org.apache.commons.beanutils.PropertyUtils;
```

```java
import java.util.Vector;

public class Teacher {
    private String name;
    private Vector certifications;

    public Teacher() {
        certifications = new Vector();
    }

    public void addCertification(String certification) {
        certifications.addElement(certification);
    }

    public String getName() {
        return name;
    }

    public void setName(String newName) {
        name = newName;
    }

    public void setCertifications(Vector certifications) {
        this.certifications = certifications;
    }

    public Vector getCertifications() {
        return certifications;
    }

    public String toString() {
        StringBuffer buf = new StringBuffer(60);
        buf.append("\nTeacher name>> " + this.getName());

        Vector certs = this.getCertifications();

        //Iterate through vector. Append content to StringBuffer.
        for (int i = 0; i < certs.size(); i++) {
            buf.append("\n\tCertification>> " + certs.get(i));
        }

        return buf.toString();
    }
}
```

The academy tag is the root tag shown in Listing 7-4. So the Academy class not only has to store the name of the academy but also references to the data held by the child tags of the academy tag. Therefore, the Academy class, shown in Listing 7-8, has two Vectors, one that will store instances of Student classes and another that will store instances of Teacher classes. So directly or indirectly you should be able to access all the data depicted in Listing 7-4 using a reference to a properly populated Academy class instance. The overridden toString method will be used later in the chapter to print the data held by an Academy instance.

Listing 7-8. Academy *Class*

```
package com.commonsbook.chap7.academy;
import org.apache.commons.beanutils.PropertyUtils;

import java.util.Vector;

public class Academy {
    private Vector students;
    private Vector teachers;
    private String name;

    public Academy() {
        students = new Vector();
        teachers = new Vector();
    }

    public void addStudent(Student student) {
        students.addElement(student);
    }

    public void addTeacher(Teacher teacher) {
        teachers.addElement(teacher);
    }

    public Vector getStudents() {
        return students;
    }

    public void setStudents(Vector newStudents) {
        students = newStudents;
    }
```

```
public Vector getTeachers() {
    return teachers;
}

public void setTeachers(Vector newTeachers) {
    teachers = newTeachers;
}

public String getName() {
    return name;
}

public void setName(String newName) {
    name = newName;
}

public String toString() {
    StringBuffer buf = new StringBuffer(60);

    buf.append("Academy name>> " + this.getName());

    Vector stud = this.getStudents();
    Vector teach = this.getTeachers();
    buf.append("\n\n**STUDENTS**");

    //Iterate through vectors. Append content to StringBuffer.
    for (int i = 0; i < stud.size(); i++) {
        buf.append(stud.get(i));
    }

    buf.append("\n\n**TEACHERS**");

    for (int i = 0; i < teach.size(); i++) {
        buf.append(teach.get(i));
    }

    return buf.toString();
}
}
```

Now that you are done with the classes that will store the data for you, you will move to the Digester code that will actually parse the XML. You will first see how you specify Digester instructions within the Java code. Next you will move these instructions out to an easily configurable XML file, making your Java code short and simple. Listing 7-9 shows the Java code to specify Digester rules and parse the XML accordingly. The thing to note in this piece of code is the use of the following rules:

- **ObjectCreate**: This rule creates a new instance of the classes Academy, Student, Teacher, and Course on a matching pattern being found.

- **SetProperties**: The SetProperties rule sets the properties of the class using the attribute values. Because the name of the attribute and the property in the class match exactly, you did not specify those details; however, if the attribute names in XML and property names in Java differ, you have to specify that mapping.

- **BeanPropertySetter**: This rule sets the properties of the bean using the values of the child tags. For example, the id and name properties of the instance of the class Course are set using this rule.

- **SetNext**: The SetNext rule moves to the next course, student, and teacher tags. You have also specified the method to call in each case.

- **CallMethod**: The CallMethod rule specifies the method to be called upon a certain pattern being found. You also specify the number of parameters that this method expects.

- **CallParam**: The CallParam rule specifies the parameter value to be passed to the method call defined using the CallMethod rule.

Listing 7-9. DigestJavaAcademy *Class (Digester Rules Defined in Java Code)*

```
package com.commonsbook.chap7.academy;
import org.apache.commons.beanutils.PropertyUtils;
import org.apache.commons.digester.Digester;

import java.util.Vector;

public class DigestJavaAcademy {
    public static void main(String[] args) throws Exception {
        DigestJavaAcademy d = new DigestJavaAcademy();
        d.digest();
    }

    public void digest() throws Exception {
        Digester digester = new Digester();
        digester.addObjectCreate("academy", Academy.class);
```

```java
//Set the attribute values as properties
digester.addSetProperties("academy");

//A new Student instance for the student tag
digester.addObjectCreate("academy/student", Student.class);

//Set the attribute values as properties
digester.addSetProperties("academy/student");

//A new Course instance
digester.addObjectCreate("academy/student/course", Course.class);

//Set properties of the Course instance with values of two child tags
digester.addBeanPropertySetter("academy/student/course/id", "id");
digester.addBeanPropertySetter("academy/student/course/name", "name");

//Next Course
digester.addSetNext("academy/student/course", "addCourse");

//Next student
digester.addSetNext("academy/student", "addStudent");

//A new instance of Teacher
digester.addObjectCreate("academy/teacher", Teacher.class);

///Set teacher name with attribute value
digester.addSetProperties("academy/teacher");

//Call Method addCertification that takes a single parameter
digester.addCallMethod("academy/teacher/certification",
    "addCertification", 1);

//Set value of the parameter for the addCertification method
digester.addCallParam("academy/teacher/certification", 0);

//Next Teacher
digester.addSetNext("academy/teacher", "addTeacher");

//Parse the XML file to get an Academy instance
Academy a = (Academy) digester.parse(this.getClass().getClassLoader()
                        .getResourceAsStream("academy.xml"));

System.out.println(a);
    }
}
```

The order in which you define rules is important. You have just represented what was obvious to you in the XML in a form that Digester can understand.

To execute this piece of code, you need to have the academy.xml file present in the CLASSPATH. Listing 7-10 shows the output upon executing this piece of code.

Listing 7-10. Output Upon Executing the Code in Listing 7-9

```
Academy name>> JAcademy

**STUDENTS**
Student name>> JavaBoy
  CourseId>>> C1  CourseName>>> JSP
  CourseId>>> C2  CourseName>>> Servlets
Student name>> JavaGirl
  CourseId>>> C3  CourseName>>> EJB

**TEACHERS**
Teacher name>> JavaGuru
  Certification>> SCJP
  Certification>> SCWCD
Teacher name>> JavaMaster
  Certification>> OCP
  Certification>> SCJP
  Certification>> SCEA
```

Looking at Listing 7-9, it is obvious that almost all the code is dedicated to configuring the Digester. Did they not teach us in school that wherever possible move all configurable items to a file that can be easily managed and manipulated? So why not do that in this case?

The org.apache.commons.digester.xmlrules package provides for an XML-based definition of Digester rules. Defining Digester rules in XML is quite simple once you get the hang of the various rules and what they do for you. Considering the more widespread nature of XML, your Digester rules are now more easily understandable to a wide variety of people involved. Even your manager might understand a thing or two!

Listing 7-11 shows the rules you defined using Java in Listing 7-9 but using XML instead.

Listing 7-11. academyRules.xml *Digester Rules Defined in XML*

```xml
<?xml version="1.0"?>
<digester-rules>
  <pattern value="academy">
      <object-create-rule classname="com.commonsbook.chap7.academy.Academy" />
```

```
        <set-properties-rule />
        <pattern value="student">
            <object-create-rule classname="com.commonsbook.chap7.academy.Student" />
            <set-properties-rule />

            <pattern value="course">
              <object-create-rule classname="com.commonsbook.chap7.academy.Course" />
              <bean-property-setter-rule pattern="id"/>
              <bean-property-setter-rule pattern="name"/>
              <set-next-rule methodname="addCourse" />
            </pattern>
            <set-next-rule methodname="addStudent" />
        </pattern>

        <pattern value="teacher">
            <object-create-rule classname="com.commonsbook.chap7.academy.Teacher" />
            <set-properties-rule />
            <call-method-rule pattern="certification" methodname="addCertification"
                paramcount="1" />
            <call-param-rule pattern="certification" paramnumber="0"/>
            <set-next-rule methodname="addTeacher" />
        </pattern>
    </pattern>
</digester-rules>
```

In the XML in Listing 7-11, the rules defined in XML almost directly map to the methods defined in the Java in Listing 7-9. All the rules now are defined using tags of that name. The easiest way to check the usage of these tags is to open the digester-rules.dtd file. You can easily find this file in the source download of the Digester component. However, even with the binary download, this file can be extracted out of commons-digester.jar file and is present in the org.apache.commons.digester.xmlrules package. You can also look at the file and Digester code using ViewCVS at http://jakarta.apache.org/site/cvsindex.html.

Document Type Definition (DTD) files define the syntax and structure of XML files, and although they take some getting used to, understanding them is not difficult.

Once you are done defining the rules in XML, the Java bit left is simple. Listing 7-12 shows the Java code where you just define the rules file to be used to create a Digester instance and then parse the XML file using that Digester instance.

Listing 7-12. DigestXMLJavaAcademy *Class (Java Code Using Rules Defined in XML)*

```java
package com.commonsbook.chap7.academy;
import java.io.File;
import java.util.Vector;
import org.apache.commons.beanutils.PropertyUtils;
import org.apache.commons.digester.Digester;
import org.apache.commons.digester.xmlrules.DigesterLoader;

public class DigestXMLJavaAcademy {

    public static void main( String[] args ) {
        DigestXMLJavaAcademy xmlDigest= new DigestXMLJavaAcademy();
        xmlDigest.digest();
    }

    public void digest(){
        try {
            //Create Digester using rules defined in academyRules.xml
            Digester digester = DigesterLoader.createDigester(
                    this.getClass().getClassLoader().getResource("academyRules.xml"));

            //Parse academy.xml using the Digester to get an instance of Academy
            Academy a = (Academy)digester.parse(
            this.getClass().getClassLoader().getResourceAsStream("academy.xml"));

            Vector vStud=a.getStudents();
            Vector vTeach=a.getTeachers();

            for (int i = 0; i < vStud.size(); i++) {
                System.out.println("Student>> "+PropertyUtils.describe(vStud.get(i)));
            }

            for (int i = 0; i < vTeach.size(); i++) {
                System.out.println("Teacher>> "+ PropertyUtils.describe(vTeach.get(i)));
            }
        } catch( Exception e ) {
            e.printStackTrace();
        }
    }
}
```

The two files academy.xml and academyRules.xml have to be present in the CLASSPATH, and upon execution of the code, you get the same output as shown in Listing 7-10 that you got using the Java code in Listing 7-9.

Introducing Other Digester Features

Apart from these Digester features, I will mention some other features of Digester:

- The Logging capability of Digester can be useful while troubleshooting. Digester uses the Commons Logging component discussed in Chapter 3. The Digester class even provides a setLogger method with which you can define the exact logger to be used.

- The org.apache.commons.digester.rss package provides an example usage of Digester to parse XML in the Rich Site Summary (RSS) format, which is widely used by news sites to provide news feeds. Most of the popular content providers support RSS, and you can find more information about RSS at http://blogs.law.harvard.edu/tech/rss/.

- You can configure Digester to validate XML using a DTD file. You should register the DTD using the register method, and you can switch on validation using the setValidating method of the Digester class.

- You can configure Digester to match patterns based on namespaces. You use the methods setNamespaceAware and setRuleNamespaceURI so that the Digester does not confuse a name tag in a namespace X with a similar name tag in a namespace Y.

Summary

In this chapter, you looked at the Digester component, which drastically cuts down on the complexity involved in parsing XML. You saw how Digester works on the simple concept of element matching patterns and how you can define rules in Java code as well as in a separate XML file. You also saw some examples that reflected common XML parsing requirements.

Using Digester and defining the rules in a separate XML file gets a big thumbs-up from me. I highly recommend Digester for all your XML parsing requirements.

#### CHAPTER 8

Using Collections and Primitives

JAVA BEGAN ITS JOURNEY without the Java Collections Framework. The Java Collections Framework was introduced in Java Development Kit (JDK) 1.2 to address the common requirement of a flexible and easy-to-use collection of objects. The Java Collections Framework introduced many classes that are used extensively in most of today's applications. The java.util package and classes such as ArrayList, HashMap, and LinkedList are all part of the Java Collections Framework.

Although the Java Collections Framework provides a lot of functionality, there are times when it is not enough. The Commons Collections component goes beyond what is offered by the Java Collections Framework and also simplifies how you work with the existing Collection classes.

Although there is some overlap between what the Commons Collections component has to offer and what the Java Collections Framework offers, there still is a lot of new and interesting stuff in the Collections component. In this chapter, you will see some of the useful and flexible classes that you can adopt for your projects. You will also look at the Primitives component, which provides collections meant for use with primitives. Table 8-1 gives the details for the components covered in this chapter.

Table 8-1. Component Details

Name	Version	Package
Collections	3.0	org.apache.commons.collections
Primitives	1.0	org.apache.commons.collections.primitives

Introducing the Collections Component

The Collections component is a nice collection of code pulled from various Jakarta projects that achieve the kind of reuse that is the goal of the Commons project. The Application Programming Interface (API) specification for the Jakarta Commons Collections component is the primary source of information for the various classes and interfaces in the component. The Collections component is a good example of the good and bad of open-source software. It has lots of cool features and functionality that make you feel indebted to the creators for the amount of time and effort they have put in; however, the component suffers from being too complex. Furthermore, the documentation, unfortunately, is not that user-friendly. Although version 3.0 is a good attempt at better organizing the contents of the component and providing more documentation, a detailed user guide and a "getting started" manual are still missing. A lot of users might just be overwhelmed by the component and never actually adopt it.

If you identify with this problem, do not plan to adopt everything there is. Decide what exactly your need or problem is, and then check whether the component offers a solution.

You can download the Collections component from `http://jakarta.apache.org/commons/collections/`. To use the component, the only requirement is JDK 1.2 or higher. Many Commons components and even other Jakarta projects use the Collections component, so it is quite likely you already have been using Collections indirectly and have the required Java Archive (JAR) file. The JAR file name was `commons-collections.jar` until version 2.1, but with 3.0 the JAR file name is now in the format `commons-collections-<version>.jar`.

Using Collections

Because the component holds different kinds of collections, utility classes, and interfaces, it is important to first classify these into different categories:

List implementations: These are implementations of the `java.util.List` interface. The `List` interface provides for an ordered collection of objects. The Java Software Development Kit (JSDK) implementations of `List` that you might be familiar with are `ArrayList`, `Vector`, and `LinkedList`. The Collections component implementations such as `FastArrayList`, `ArrayStack`, and `CursorableLinkedList` try to provide faster and easier options than the JSDK implementations. The package `org.apache.commons.collections.list` contains all the `List` implementations.

Map implementations: These are implementations of the `java.util.Map` interface. The `Map` interface provides for key/value pairs. The keys are unique, and one key can map to only one object. The commonly used JSDK implementations of `Map` are `HashMap`, `Hashtable`, `Properties`, and `TreeMap`. `BeanMap`, `ExtendedProperties`, `FastHashMap`, `FastTreeMap`, `LRUMap`, `MultiHashMap`, `ProxyMap`, `ReferenceMap`. `SequencedHashMap`, `SoftRefHashMap`, and `StaticBucketMap` are some of the implementations for the `Map` interface provided by the Collections component. Although the package `org.apache.commons.collections.map` contains most implementations of `Map`, there are some implementations such as `BeanMap`, `ExtendedProperties`, `FastHashMap`, and `FastTreeMap` that are being carried forward from version 2.1 and still exist in the package `org.apache.commons.collections`.

BidiMap implementations: Collections 3.0 has introduced a new interface: BidiMap. BidiMap provides bidirectional lookup, so you can look up not only the value using the key but can also the key using the value. DualHashBidiMap, DualTreeBidiMap, and TreeBidiMap are the implementations of BidiMap provided in the package org.apache.commons.collections.bidimap

Buffer implementations: org.apache.commons.collections.Buffer is an interface introduced in version 2.1 by the Collections component. The Buffer interface extends the java.util.Collection interface and provides for objects to be removed in a specific order. The Buffer implementations provided in the package org.apache.commons.collections.buffer are PriorityBuffer, BoundedFifoBuffer, CircularFifoBuffer, and UnboundedFifoBuffer. ArrayStack is the only Buffer implementation that exists in the package org.apache.commons.collections and that hasn't been deprecated.

Bag implementations: org.apache.commons.collections.Bag is another interface introduced in version 2.1 of the Collections component. Bag implementations keep a count of how many times an object appears in the collection. HashBag and TreeBag are Bag implementations provided in the package org.apache.commons.collections.bag. The SortedBag interface extends the Bag interface and maintains a sorted order among its unique representative members. TreeBag is an implementation of SortedBag.

Utilities: These are utility classes for various implementations. These classes are perhaps the easiest and most useful offerings of the component. The classes BagUtils, BufferUtils, ClosureUtils, CollectionUtils, ComparatorUtils, EnumerationUtils, FactoryUtils, IteratorUtils, ListUtils, MapUtils, PredicateUtils, SetUtils, and TransformerUtils all provide static methods that simplify many collection-related tasks.

The Collections 3.0 component was recently released; the following list shows how the new version differs from version 2.1:

Changed package structure: Version 3.0 offers a more systematic package organization than version 2.1. Packages are based on the interface names being implemented, so the org.apache.commons.collections.list package consists only of List implementations.

Bidirectional maps: Bidirectional maps will be introduced with the new interface org.apache.commons.collections.BidiMap. BidiMap extends Map, so it has the Map functionality, and it also adds the capability to easily look up values based on keys as well as keys based on values.

New MapIterator: There is a new `MapIterator` interface meant to simplify iterating over a `Map`. This interface has methods you can use to easily fetch key and values.

New ResettableIterator: `ResettableIterator` can make `Iterator` reuse possible because it has the capability to reset the `Iterator` to an initial state.

Deprecated interface: The `PriorityQueue` interface has been deprecated. Also, the `PriorityQueue` implementation `org.apache.commons.collections.BinaryHeap` has been deprecated and will be replaced by `org.apache.commons.collections.buffer.PriorityBuffer`.

Deprecated classes: The following classes in the package `org.apache.commons.collections` have been deprecated in most cases because they have been moved to a more appropriate package based on their implementation: `BinaryHeap`, `BoundedFifoBuffer`, `CursorableLinkedList`, `DefaultMapBag`, `DefaultMapEntry`, `DoubleOrderedMap`, `HashBag`, `LRUMap`, `ProxyMap`, `ReferenceMap`, `SequencedHashMap`, `StaticBucketMap`, `SynchronizedPriorityQueue`, `TreeBag`, and `UnboundedFifoBuffer`.

New abstract classes: `AbstractHashedMap` and `AbstractLinkedMap` are subclassed to create new hash-based and hash link–based maps.

List Implementations

The interface `java.util.List` represents an ordered collection that is also known as a *sequence*. All implementations of the `List` interface give the user control over where exactly a particular object can be placed. Whenever you use `List` implementations such as an `ArrayList` or a `Vector`, you can specify an index where the object should be placed, and while retrieving objects, you can specify the index from where the object should be fetched.

The `List` implementations in the Collections component are in the package `org.apache.commons.collections.list`. Apart from implementations such as `CursorableLinkedList` and `NodeCachingLinkedList`, some decorators also exist in the package.

NOTE *The decorator design pattern provides a flexible way to add behavior to a class without subclassing it. In most packages in the Collections component, you will find some implementations and some decorators.*

The decorators in the List package are as follows:

- **SynchronizedList**: This class decorates a List to synchronize method access.

- **UnmodifiableList**: This List cannot be modified.

- **PredicatedList**: Only elements that are valid as per an implementation of the interface org.apache.commons.collections.Predicate can be added to this List. The constructor of this class takes a List and a Predicate as input.

- **TypedList**: Only elements of a specific type can be added to this List.

- **TransformedList**: Transforms all objects added to the List using a Transformer interface implementation. I will discuss Transformer later in the "Utilities" section.

- **FixedSizeList**: The List has a fixed size.

- **LazyList**: The LazyList decorator is an interesting addition that can use a Factory to create new objects on demand. The constructor takes a java.util.List implementation and org.apache.commons.collections. Factory implementation as input.

- **SetUniqueList**: This is a list that, like java.util.Set, ensures that there are no duplicates.

The ArrayStack class present in the package org.apache.commons.collections is very much a List; however, it also implements the Buffer interface. You will learn about ArrayStack later in this chapter. CursorableLinkedList is a doubly linked list that implements all the optional List operations, and like java.util.LinkedList, the CursorableLinkedList implementation can be used as a stack, queue, or double-ended queue (*deque*).

You can probably find a use for the FastArrayList class right away. This class extends java.util.ArrayList and introduces an interesting concept of working in *fast mode* or *slow mode*. If you are wondering why anybody would want a class to perform slowly when there is a fast option, there is a sensible reason for that.

FastArrayList has been created to work in a multithreaded environment where the majority of method calls are read-only, so FastArrayList is optimized to perform better than java.util.ArrayList in such an environment. Therefore, in fast mode, all read calls are nonsynchronized. If you do write to the FastArrayList while it is in fast mode, you perform the following steps as stated in the Javadocs:

1. Clone the existing collection.

2. Perform the modification on the clone.

3. Replace the existing collection with the (modified) clone.

On creation, the FastArrayList is in slow mode. In this mode, all access is synchronized. The expected usage is to populate your FastArrayList in slow mode and then switch to fast mode when you expect only read functionality.

Note that the creators of FastArrayList say that the class might cause unexpected problems on some architectures. See the Javadocs for details of when these problems might occur. They also recommend using a standard java.util.ArrayList instead of FastArrayList if only a single thread will be using the ArrayList.

You will now see an example where you time an ArrayList and a FastArrayList in slow and fast mode. In Listing 8-1, you create a new FastArrayList and ArrayList, add a million strings to them, and then get back those values. You use new String to create strings to prevent the Java Virtual Machine (JVM) from reusing string instances.

Listing 8-1. FastArrayListTrial

```
package com.commonsbook.chap8;
import org.apache.commons.collections.FastArrayList;

import java.util.ArrayList;

public class FastArrayListTrial {
    public static void main(String[] args) {
        //create a new FastArrayList and ArrrayList
        FastArrayList fArList = new FastArrayList();
        ArrayList arList = new ArrayList();

        //Add a million strings to the list
        //Use new String to stop JVM from reusing String instances
        for (int i = 0; i < 1000000; i++) {
            fArList.add(new String("AString"));
            arList.add(new String("AString"));
        }

        //Get time in milliseconds
        long utilBegin = System.currentTimeMillis();

        for (int util = 0; util < 1000000; util++) {
            fArList.get(util);
        }
```

```
        System.out.println("UTIL ArrayList Milliseconds Taken = " +
            (System.currentTimeMillis() - utilBegin));


        long slowBegin = System.currentTimeMillis();


        for (int slow = 0; slow < 1000000; slow++) {
            fArList.get(slow);
        }


        System.out.println("SLOW FastArrayList Milliseconds Taken = " +
            (System.currentTimeMillis() - slowBegin));


        fArList.setFast(true);


        long fastBegin = System.currentTimeMillis();


        for (int fast = 0; fast < 100000; fast++) {
            fArList.get(fast);
        }


        System.out.println("FAST FastArrayList Milliseconds Taken = " +
            (System.currentTimeMillis() - fastBegin));
    }
}
```

The output upon execution on a Pentium 4 with 512 megabytes (MB) of Random Access Memory (RAM) was as follows (the output will vary based on your machine configuration):

```
UIIL ArrayList Milliseconds Taken = 187
SLOW FastArrayList Milliseconds Taken = 188
FAST FastArrayList Milliseconds Taken = 0
```

So, the FastArrayList does actually work quite fast when it is working in the fast mode and is used for only read access. Note that this example does not demonstrate how these classes work in a multithreaded application. The time differences in that case would be even more significant.

Map Implementations

All Map implementations have the capability to hold key/value pairs of data. Each key in a Map is unique and can map to, at most, one value. You use Map quite regularly in Java applications in the form of HashMap, Hashtable, Properties, and so on.

In the same way that the `Properties` class is a specialized class for using
`*.properties` files, the Collections component aims at providing specialized
maps that serve specific purposes.

The `org.apache.commons.collections.BeanMap` class is a `Map` implementation
for JavaBeans. It maintains key/value pairs where the property names in the bean
are the keys and the property values are the values in the key/value pair. You will
now see an example where you create a bean and fetch property values using
a `BeanMap`. Listing 8-2 shows a class `Human` that has two properties: name and age.

Listing 8-2. Human *Class*

```java
package com.commonsbook.chap8;
public class Human {
    private String name;
    private int age;

    Human() {
    }

    Human(String name, int age) {
        this.name = name;
        this.age = age;
    }

    public void setName(String name) {
        this.name = name;
    }

    public String getName() {
        return name;
    }

    public void setAge(int age) {
        this.age = age;
    }

    public int getAge() {
        return age;
    }

    public String toString() {
        return "Name = " + this.name + " \tAge= " + this.age;
    }
}
```

You would normally fetch the property values using the getter methods provided. Listing 8-3 shows how you can do that using a BeanMap.

Listing 8-3. BeanMapTrial *Class*

```
package com.commonsbook.chap8;
import org.apache.commons.collections.BeanMap;

public class BeanMapTrial {
    public static void main(String[] args) {
        Human one = new Human();
        one.setAge(100);
        one.setName("Anonymous");

        BeanMap humanBeanMap = new BeanMap(one);
        System.out.println("Name Type >>" + humanBeanMap.getType("name"));
        System.out.println("Name Class >>" + humanBeanMap.get("name").getClass());
        System.out.println("Name Value >>" + humanBeanMap.get("name"));

        System.out.println("Age Type >>" + humanBeanMap.getType("age"));
        System.out.println("Age Class >>" + humanBeanMap.get("age").getClass());
        System.out.println("Age Value >>" + humanBeanMap.get("age"));
    }
}
```

In BeanMapTrial you create a new instance of Human and then create a BeanMap using that instance. The output upon execution is as follows:

```
Name Type >>class java.lang.String
Name Class >>class java.lang.String
Name Value >>Anonymous
Age Type >>int
Age Class >>class java.lang.Integer
Age Value >>100
```

The thing to note is that because a Map can hold only objects and not primitives, the age property that is int gets converted to an Integer instance.

As the name suggests, the ExtendedProperties class is an extension of the standard java.util.Properties class. The ExtendedProperties class extends Hashtable and not the class Properties. The ExtendedProperties class provides the standard features of the Properties file and adds a feature of repeating the same key many times in the properties file. So with ExtendedProperties, you can have the properties file contents as follows:

```
productsoffered = books
productsoffered = music
productsoffered = gadgets
```

The property value that would actually be created is as follows:

```
productsoffered = books, productsoffered, gadgets
```

The `ExtendedProperties` class separates the values using the comma as a token.

The `FastHashMap` and `FastTreeMap` classes work similarly to the `FastArrayList` you saw earlier in the chapter. These classes work in fast and slow modes and provide efficient alternatives to `java.util.HashMap` and `java.util.TreeMap`.

`LRUMap` is another `Map` implementation. `LRU` stands for Least Recently Used, and this implementation uses the LRU algorithm to remove items from the `Map` when the maximum size is reached and new items are added. The `MultiHashMap` is an implementation of the `MultiMap` interface, and instead of returning an `Object`, it returns a `Collection` on every call to the get method. So collections in a `Map` get you a table-like structure with which to work. To add a new object to a particular collection, you now just have to say `map.put("foo", "Bar")`. You do not need to get a `Collection` using `map.get("foo")` and then add to the `Collection` using `collection.add("bar")`. `Map` implementations provided in the package `org.apache.commons.collections.map` are as follows:

- **HashedMap**: This is an improved version of the standard `java.util.HashMap` that provides the `MapIterator` functionality.

- **IdentityMap**: This `Map` matches keys and values using `==` instead of the `equals` method.

- **Flat3Map**: This `Map` works many times faster than `HashMap` for size 3 and smaller.

- **LinkedMap**: This `Map` maintains the insertion order.

- **ReferenceMap**: With this `Map`, the garbage collector can remove mappings if a key or value becomes unreachable.

- **StaticBucketMap**: This is an efficient and thread-safe `Map`.

The decorators provided in the package `org.apache.commons.collections.map` are `UnmodifiableMap`, `PredicatedMap`, `TypedMap`, `TransformedMap`, `FixedSizeMap`, `LazyMap`, and `ListOrderedMap`.

BidiMap Implementations

The org.apache.commons.collections.BidiMap interface that provides a bidirectional map is introduced in version 3.0 and is implemented by the classes DualHashBidiMap, DualTreeBidiMap, and TreeBidiMap in the package org.apache.commons.collections.bidimap. Because the BidiMap interface extends the Map interface, any BidiMap is very much a Map. The purpose of a BidiMap is that you can look up not only the value using the key but also the key using the value.

DualHashBidiMap uses two HashMap instances for the implementation, and DualTreeBidiMap uses two TreeMap instances. In Listing 8-4, you create a new TreeBidiMap and also use the new MapIterator introduced in Collections 3.0.

Listing 8-4. BidiMapTrial

```
package com.commonsbook.chap8;
import org.apache.commons.collections.MapIterator;
import org.apache.commons.collections.bidimap.TreeBidiMap;

public class TreeBidiMapTrial {
    public static void main(String[] args) {
        TreeBidiMap tbm = new TreeBidiMap();
        tbm.put("KEY1", "VALUE1");
        tbm.put("KEY2", "VALUE2");

        System.out.println("Value for KEY2 >>" + tbm.get("KEY2"));
        System.out.println("Key for VALUE2 >>" + tbm.getKey("VALUE2"));

        System.out.println("***Iterate over Map***");

        MapIterator it = tbm.mapIterator();

        while (it.hasNext()) {
            System.out.println("Key=" + it.next() + "\nVal=" + it.getValue());
        }
    }
}
```

In this example, you create a new TreeBidiMap and insert two key/value pairs into the TreeBidiMap. Next, you use the get method to get the value for the key provided and then the getKey method to get the key for the value provided. You then get a MapIterator and use the methods of the MapIterator to get data far more easily than using a standard Iterator. The output upon the execution of this code is as follows:

```
Value for KEY2 >>VALUE2
Key for VALUE2 >>KEY2
***Iterate over Map***
Key=KEY1
Val=VALUE1
Key=KEY2
Val=VALUE2
```

Buffer Implementations

The org.apache.commons.collections.Buffer interface extends the java.util.
Collection interface and allows objects to be removed in a well-defined removal
order. The interface defines the following two methods:

- **Object get()**: This method returns the next object in the buffer without
  removing it from the buffer.

- **Object remove()**: This method returns the next object from the buffer but
  also removes it from the buffer.

UnboundedFifoBuffer and BoundedFifoBuffer are efficient implementations of
the Buffer interface in the package org.apache.commons.collections.buffer. Both
these classes follow the First In First Out (FIFO) format, so the removal order is
based on the insertion order. Listing 8-5 shows how to use these classes.

Listing 8-5. FifoBufferTrial *Class*

```
package com.commonsbook.chap8;
import org.apache.commons.collections.buffer.BoundedFifoBuffer;
import org.apache.commons.collections.buffer.UnboundedFifoBuffer;
public class FifoBufferTrial {
    public static void main(String[] args) {
        BoundedFifoBuffer bFifoBuffer = new BoundedFifoBuffer(3);
        bFifoBuffer.add("B One");
        bFifoBuffer.add("B Two");
        bFifoBuffer.add("B Three");

        System.out.println("Bounded Get >>" + bFifoBuffer.get());
        System.out.println("Bounded Remove >>" + bFifoBuffer.remove());
        System.out.println("Bounded Remove >>" + bFifoBuffer.remove());
        System.out.println("Bounded Size >>" + bFifoBuffer.size());
```

```
UnboundedFifoBuffer unbFifoBuffer = new UnboundedFifoBuffer(1);
unbFifoBuffer.add("UB One");
unbFifoBuffer.add("UB Two");
unbFifoBuffer.add("UB Three");

System.out.println("\nUnbounded Get >>" + unbFifoBuffer.get());
System.out.println("Unbounded Remove >>" + unbFifoBuffer.remove());
System.out.println("Unbounded Remove >>" + unbFifoBuffer.remove());
System.out.println("Unbounded Size >>" + unbFifoBuffer.size());
    }
}
```

The output upon executing the class `FifoBufferTrial` is as follows:

```
Bounded Get >>B One
Bounded Remove >>B One
Bounded Remove >>B Two
Bounded Size >>1

Unbounded Get >>UB One
Unbounded Remove >>UB One
Unbounded Remove >>UB Two
Unbounded Size >>1
```

While instantiating a new `BoundedFifoBuffer`, you specify the size as 3 because you will get a `BufferOverflowException` if you specify any size less than 3 and yet insert three objects. However, in the case of an `UnboundedFifoBuffer`, you get no exception even when you specify the size as 1 but add three objects. This is possible because, unlike a `BoundedFifoBuffer`, an `UnboundedFifoBuffer` is capable of altering the size of the buffer at runtime.

The `ArrayStack` class is a `Buffer` implementation that also implements the `java.util.Stack` API. `ArrayStack` extends `ArrayList` and is unsynchronized. As with any stack, the removal order is based on the insertion order, so whatever is entered last is removed first; this is Last In First Out (LIFO). However, the `Iterator` for `ArrayStack` returns elements in a bottom-up form where the first object entered is the first object returned.

NOTE *For anyone not aware of what the* stack *data structure is, think of how you stack books on a table. The first book you put on the table is at the bottom of the stack, and the last one is at the top. The only way to get to the book at the bottom is to first remove all the books on top of it.*

Listing 8-6 shows how to use ArrayStack.

Listing 8-6. ArrayStackTrial

```
package com.commonsbook.chap8;
import org.apache.commons.collections.ArrayStack;

import java.util.Iterator;

public class ArrayStackTrial {
    public static void main(String[] args) {
        ArrayStack aStack = new ArrayStack();
        aStack.add("STOne");
        aStack.add("STTwo");
        aStack.add("STThree");

        Iterator stackItr = aStack.iterator();

        while (stackItr.hasNext()) {
            System.out.println("**" + stackItr.next());
        }

        System.out.println(">>" + aStack.remove());
        System.out.println(">>" + aStack.remove());
        System.out.println(">>" + aStack.remove());
    }
}
```

The output upon executing ArrayStackTrial is as follows:

```
**STOne
**STTwo
**STThree
>>STThree
>>STTwo
>>STOne
```

The thing to note here is that the first object returned by the Iterator is STOne, and the one returned by the remove method is STThree.

The PriorityBuffer class in version 3.0 replaces the BinaryHeap class that existed until version 2.1. PriorityBuffer implements the Buffer interface, and the removal order of elements from a PriorityBuffer depends on the natural sort order of the elements or on the Comparator provided. The java.util.Comparator interface defines two methods: compare and equals. Implementations of the Comparator interface compare two objects of the same class.

Listing 8-7 shows an example where you create two `PriorityBuffer` instances and shows how the elements get sorted based on the natural order and based on a `Comparator`. You will use the same `Human` class you used in Listing 8-2. Listing 8-8 shows a class `HumanComparator` that implements the `Comparator` interface and provides a `compare` method. The `compare` method in `HumanComparator` compares two instances of the `Human` class.

Listing 8-7. PriorityBufferTrial

```
package com.commonsbook.chap8;
import org.apache.commons.collections.buffer.PriorityBuffer;

public class PriorityBufferTrial {
    public static void main(String[] args) {
        PriorityBuffer bHeapOne = new PriorityBuffer();
        bHeapOne.add(new Integer(44));
        bHeapOne.add(new Integer(11));
        bHeapOne.add(new Integer(99));

        System.out.println(">>" + bHeapOne.remove());
        System.out.println(">>" + bHeapOne.remove());
        System.out.println(">>" + bHeapOne.remove());

        PriorityBuffer bHeapTwo = new PriorityBuffer(new HumanComparator());
        bHeapTwo.add(new Human("HumanTwo", 22));
        bHeapTwo.add(new Human("HumanOne", 11));
        bHeapTwo.add(new Human("HumanThree", 33));

        System.out.println("##" + bHeapTwo.remove());
        System.out.println("##" + bHeapTwo.remove());
        System.out.println("##" + bHeapTwo.remove());
    }
}
```

Listing 8-8. `HumanComparator` *Class*

```
package com.commonsbook.chap8;
import java.util.Comparator;

public class HumanComparator implements Comparator {
    public int compare(Object humanOne, Object humanTwo) {
        if (!(humanOne instanceof Human) || !(humanTwo instanceof Human)) {
            throw new ClassCastException("A Human object expected.");
        }
```

```
        int diff = ((Human) humanOne).getAge() - ((Human) humanTwo).getAge();

        return diff;
    }
}
```

The output upon executing the code in Listing 8-7 is as follows:

```
>>11
>>44
>>99
##Name = HumanOne    Age= 11
##Name = HumanTwo    Age= 22
##Name = HumanThree    Age= 33
```

The output shows that although the integers were sorted in their natural order, the Human objects were sorted based on the value of the age property and using the Comparator you provided. Note that the Iterator you could get on the PriorityBuffer will not return objects in any specific order.

Bag Implementations

The org.apache.commons.collections.Bag interface extends java.util.Collection, and implementations of Bag are expected to count the number of times an object appears in a collection. The Bag interface defines 11 methods. Note that some of these methods violate the Collection contract and do not behave in the fashion specified by the Collection interface.

HashBag and TreeBag are two implementations of Bag that are provided by the Collections component. Both HashBag and TreeMap extend AbstractMapBag and build on the basic implementation provided by AbstractMapBag. Listing 8-9 shows an example of HashBag usage where you add multiple copies of objects of the class Human as shown in Listing 8-2 and then get a count of these objects. It also uses the uniqueSet method of the Bag interface to get a java.util.Set of objects that are unique.

Listing 8-9. HashBagTrial *Class*

```
package com.commonsbook.chap8;
import org.apache.commons.collections.bag.HashBag;

import java.util.Iterator;
import java.util.Set;
```

```
public class HashBagTrial {
    public static void main(String[] args) {
        HashBag hBag = new HashBag();
        Human h1 = new Human("One", 22);
        Human h2 = new Human("Two", 32);

        hBag.add(h1, 5);

        hBag.add(h2);
        h2.setAge(44);
        hBag.add(h2);

        System.out.println("h1 count>>" + hBag.getCount(h1));
        System.out.println("h2 count>>" + hBag.getCount(h2));

        Set uSet = hBag.uniqueSet();
        Iterator uSetItr = uSet.iterator();

        while (uSetItr.hasNext()) {
            System.out.println(uSetItr.next());
        }
    }
}
```

In this code, you first add five copies of the object h1 and then add two copies of h2. The output upon execution is as follows:

```
h1 count>>5
h2 count>>2
Name = Two   Age= 44
Name = One   Age= 22
```

Note that despite adding many objects and even editing the value of the property age, the unique set still returns only two objects.

Utilities

The utility classes are quite useful even if you do not intend to adopt any of the Collections component classes discussed so far and intend to stick with the java.util classes. The utility classes are BagUtils, BufferUtils, ClosureUtils, CollectionUtils, ComparatorUtils, EnumerationUtils, FactoryUtils, IteratorUtils, ListUtils, MapUtils, PredicateUtils, SetUtils, and TransformerUtils. The names of all the classes suggest the kind of collections to which these utility classes cater.

The `CollectionUtils` class provides many static methods that do useful things, including adding all elements from another collection, `Enumeration`, or `Iterator`; adding an `Object` array to a collection; checking if one collection contains any elements from another; subtracting one collection from another; creating a union of two collections; reversing an array; and finding elements from a collection based on an implementation of the `Predicate` interface. However, one feature I found particularly impressive was that of transforming collections.

The `org.apache.commons.collections.Transformer` interface defines a single method: `Object transform(Object input)`. You provide an implementation of `Transformer` to the methods of the `CollectionUtils` class, and you can transform the entire collection based on what logic is present in the `Transformer`. You will now see an example where you write and use a `Transformer` that increments all `Integer` values by ten. Listing 8-10 shows such an example where the class `TenPlusTransformer` implements `Transformer` and the method `transform` increments `Integer` values by ten. The `collect` method of `CollectionUtils` does the job for you and returns a new `List` that has all `Integer` values incremented by ten.

Listing 8-10. `CollectionUtilsTrial` *Class*

```
package com.commonsbook.chap8;
import org.apache.commons.collections.CollectionUtils;
import org.apache.commons.collections.Transformer;

import java.util.ArrayList;
import java.util.Collection;
import java.util.Iterator;

public class CollectionUtilsTrial {
    public static void main(String[] args) {
        ArrayList integerList = new ArrayList();
        integerList.add(new Integer(10));
        integerList.add(new Integer(11));
        integerList.add(new Integer(12));

        System.out.println("Old >>" + integerList);

        Collection incrementedList = CollectionUtils.collect(integerList,
                new TenPlusTransformer());
        System.out.println("Transformed >>" + incrementedList);
    }
}
```

```
class TenPlusTransformer implements Transformer {
    public Object transform(Object input) {
        if (!(input instanceof Integer)) {
            throw new ClassCastException("An Integer object expected. ");
        }

        //increment input value by 10
        return new Integer(((Integer) input).intValue() + 10);
    }
}
```

The output upon execution of is as follows; it shows that the Human objects
were sorted using the Comparator provided:

```
Old >>[10, 11, 12]
Transformed >>[20, 21, 22]
```

In Listing 8-7 you already saw how you could use the Comparator interface to
compare objects; the ComparatorUtils class can make it even easier. In Listing 8-11,
you use the class BinaryHeapTrial that implements Comparator as shown in
Listing 8-7.

Listing 8-11. ComparatorUtilsTrial *Class*

```
package com.commonsbook.chap8;
import org.apache.commons.collections.ComparatorUtils;

import java.util.Comparator;

public class ComparatorUtilsTrial {
    public static void main(String[] args) {
        Human one = new Human("HumanTwo", 22);
        Human two = null;
        Human three = new Human("HumanThree", 33);

        //Get Comparator that treats a null value as higher than a non-null value
        Comparator cn = ComparatorUtils.nullHighComparator(new HumanComparator());
        Human maxHuman = (Human) ComparatorUtils.max(one, two, cn);
        Human minHuman = (Human) ComparatorUtils.min(one, two, cn);
        System.out.println("** MAX IS >>" + maxHuman);
        System.out.println("** MIN IS >>" + minHuman);
```

```
        //Get Comparator that will reverse the comparator logic
        Comparator rev = ComparatorUtils.reversedComparator(new HumanComparator());
        Human revMaxHuman = (Human) ComparatorUtils.max(one, three, rev);
        Human revMinHuman = (Human) ComparatorUtils.min(one, three, rev);
        System.out.println("## REV MAX IS >>" + revMaxHuman);
        System.out.println("## REV MIN IS >>" + revMinHuman);
    }
}
```

The `nullHighComparator` method gives you a modified `Comparator` that treats a `null` value as higher than any non-`null` value. So the output upon execution is as follows; it shows a `null` as the maximum value and the `Human` object as the minimum value. The `reversedComparator` method will reverse the comparator logic. So, as shown in the following output, the `max` method now returns the minimum of the two values:

```
** MAX IS >>null
** MIN IS >>Name = HumanTwo    Age= 22
## REV MAX IS >>Name = HumanTwo    Age= 22
## REV MIN IS >>Name = HumanThree    Age= 33
```

The other three utility classes—`ListUtils`, `MapUtils`, and `SetUtils`—all provide useful methods to work with `List`, `Map`, and `Set`, respectively. The `MapUtils` in particular has methods such as `getFloat`, `getByte`, and `getDouble` that can eliminate the task of having to cast objects, which you need to do with all versions prior to JSDK 1.5. You can also return a default value if the data type conversion fails.

The `IteratorUtils` class is meant to simplify iteration-related tasks. Listing 8-12 shows an example where you use some of the features of `IterationUtils`.

Listing 8-12. `IterationUtilsTrial`

```java
package com.commonsbook.chap8;
import org.apache.commons.collections.IteratorUtils;

import java.util.Iterator;
import java.util.List;

public class IteratorUtilsTrial {
    public static void main(String[] args) {
        String[] weekDays = new String[] { "Mon", "Tue", "Wed", "Thu", "Fri" };
        Iterator daysItr = IteratorUtils.arrayIterator(weekDays, 1, 3);

        while (daysItr.hasNext()) {
            System.out.println("## itr =" + daysItr.next());
        }
```

```
Iterator daysItr1 = IteratorUtils.arrayIterator(weekDays, 2);
List daysList = IteratorUtils.toList(daysItr1);

for (int i = 0; i < daysList.size(); i++) {
    System.out.println(">> list =" + daysList.get(i));
}
    }
}
```

In this example, you first get an Iterator for elements in the array weekDays, starting with the index 1 and ending with 3. You later get an Iterator for elements starting with index 2 and then get a List from this Iterator. The output upon execution is as follows:

```
## itr =Tue
## itr =Wed
>> list =Wed
>> list =Thu
>> list =Fri
```

You will now look at the Primitives component, which provides similar capabilities to what you have seen so far but only for Java primitives.

Introducing Primitives

The java.util package has been around for quite a while now, and most of you are pretty used to using only objects while working with collections. Using primitives is a strict no-no because none of the collections can directly store primitives. You always need to use a wrapper class such as Byte, Char, Short, Integer, Long, Float, or Double to wrap the primitives byte, char, short, int, long, float, and double, respectively. You probably cannot help but wonder why a simple option does not exist so that you can maintain a collection of primitives. Because the basic java.util package has not obliged and provided primitive collections, the Primitives component has to step in and do that job. The big advantage for a Primitives collection over a standard collection is that a standard java.util.ArrayList of java.lang.Byte will take up 16 bytes per element but a Primitives ArrayByteList will take only 1 byte per element. With JSDK 1.5, you will be able to have collections of primitives, but the Primitives component alternatives will still take only a fraction of the size of JSDK 1.5 primitive collections. You can download the Primitives component from http://jakarta.apache.org/commons/primitives/.

The Primitives component provides collections similar to the collections you usually use with objects. The component provides similar capabilities for all primitives. This section covers int and shows what you can do with int collections.

The interfaces related to int are IntCollection, IntIterator, IntList, and IntListIterator. RandomAccessIntList implements the IntCollection and IntList interfaces and provides an abstract base class for IntList implementations. ArrayIntList is the actual implementation you will use in Listing 8-13. ArrayIntList is a list backed by an array of int.

Listing 8-13. UseIntPrimitive *Class*

```
package com.commonsbook.chap8;
import org.apache.commons.collections.primitives.ArrayIntList;
import org.apache.commons.collections.primitives.IntIterator;

public class UseIntPrimitive {
    public static void main(String[] args) {
        ArrayIntList aIntList = new ArrayIntList();
        aIntList.add(1);
        aIntList.add(2);

        IntIterator intItr = aIntList.iterator();

        while (intItr.hasNext()) {
            System.out.println(">> " + intItr.next());
        }

        //Set 8 at index 1
        aIntList.set(1, 8);
        System.out.println("Value at index 1 >>" + aIntList.get(1));
    }
}
```

The output upon executing the code shown in Listing 8-13 is as follows:

```
>> 1
>> 2
Value at index 1 >>8
```

So, not only can you easily maintain collections of primitives, but you also can use Iterator and most of the other features that you would usually use while working with java.util collections. Similarly to int, the Primitives component provides classes and interfaces for all the other primitives.

Summary

In this chapter, you looked at the Collections and Primitives components. Both these components can be quite useful on projects and are relevant to every kind of Java development you might undertake. The Primitives component is straight-forward and easy to use, but Collections does have its complex areas.

I recommend you use the tools and utilities provided in these components but also suggest you look at these components with respect to a specific need or problem that you have to solve rather than trying to use everything they offer.

CHAPTER 9

Using HttpClient and FileUpload

ALL COMMUNICATION OVER THE INTERNET happens using a standard set of protocols, such as File Transfer Protocol (FTP), Simple Mail Transfer Protocol (SMTP), Post Office Protocol (POP), Hypertext Transfer Protocol (HTTP), and so on. HTTP is one of the most popular of these protocols and is integral to the World Wide Web. It is also a protocol that many of today's applications have to be aware of and use wisely. If a Java application has to interact using HTTP, the Commons HttpClient component can make things a bit easier. Using this component, you do not have to worry about all the technicalities of the protocol but just concern yourself with the various classes and methods provided by the HttpClient component. This chapter covers the capabilities of the HttpClient component and provides some hands-on examples.

The chapter also covers the FileUpload component, which simplifies file-upload tasks on the server side. Finally, you will work through an example where you use HttpClient and FileUpload together.

 NOTE *For all server-based examples in this chapter, I have used Tomcat version 4.0.6; however, you should not have any problems if you use another server that supports servlets and Java Server Page (JSP) technology.*

Table 9-1 shows the details for the components covered in this chapter.

Table 9-1. Component Details

Name	Version	Package
HttpClient	2.0-rc1	`org.apache.commons.httpclient`
FileUpload	1.0	`org.apache.commons.fileupload`

Introducing HttpClient

HttpClient is an attempt to provide a simple Application Programming Interface (API) that Java developers can use to create code that communicates over HTTP. If you are developing a Web browser or just an application that occasionally needs some data from the Web, HttpClient can help you develop the client code that will communicate over HTTP. As the name suggests, HttpClient is meant only for HTTP client code and cannot be used to, say, develop a server that processes HTTP requests.

I recommend you use HttpClient instead of using the java.net classes because HttpClient is easier to work with, it supports some HTTP features that java.net does not, and it has a vibrant community backing it. Visit http://www.nogoop.com/product_16. html#compare to compare HttpClient, java.net, and a couple of other APIs.

With a number of Commons components, the Javadocs are the only real documentation that exists. However, with HttpClient some good documentation exists beyond the Javadocs. A short tutorial at http://jakarta.apache.org/commons/ httpclient/tutorial.html can get you started with HttpClient.

These are some of the important features of HttpClient:

- Implements HTTP versions 1.0 and 1.1

- Implements all HTTP methods, such as GET, POST, PUT, DELETE, HEAD, OPTIONS, and TRACE

- Supports communication using HTTPS and connections through HTTP proxies

- Supports authentication using Basic, Digest, and NT LAN Manager (NTLM) methods

- Handles cookies

You will now see the various elements of the HttpClient component and how they fall into place to get you talking over HTTP.

Using HttpClient

HttpClient uses the Commons Logging component, so the only dependency for HttpClient to work properly is that the commons-logging component Java Archive (JAR) file be present. Using HttpClient to handle most requirements is fairly simple. You just need to understand a few key classes and interfaces. The following sections present a simple example of sending a GET request and then explain the classes that play a role in how the example works.

Using the GET Method

The GET method is the most common method used to send an HTTP request. Every time you click a hyperlink, you send an HTTP request using the GET method. In Chapter 4, which covered the Validator component, you saw an example where, upon successful submission of a Hypertext Markup Language (HTML) form containing the three fields firstname, lastname, and email, you received a page stating that the submission was successful, as shown in Figure 4-3. You will see the same example here, but you will now invoke it using not the Web browser but just HttpClient-based Java code (see Listing 9-1).

Listing 9-1. HttpClientTrial

```java
package com.commonsbook.chap9;
import java.io.FileOutputStream;
import java.io.IOException;
import org.apache.commons.httpclient.*;
import org.apache.commons.httpclient.methods.GetMethod;

public class SubmitHttpForm {

    private static String url =
        "http://localhost:8080/validatorStrutsApp/userInfo.do";

    public static void main(String[] args) {

        //Instantiate an HttpClient
        HttpClient client = new HttpClient();

        //Instantiate a GET HTTP method
        HttpMethod method = new GetMethod(url);

        //Define name-value pairs to set into the QueryString
        NameValuePair nvp1= new NameValuePair("firstName","fname");
        NameValuePair nvp2= new NameValuePair("lastName","lname");
        NameValuePair nvp3= new NameValuePair("email","email@email.com");

        method.setQueryString(new NameValuePair[]{nvp1,nvp2, nvp3});

        try{
            int statusCode = client.executeMethod(method);
```

```
        System.out.println("QueryString>>> "+method.getQueryString());
        System.out.println("Status Text>>>"
                +HttpStatus.getStatusText(statusCode));

        //Get data as a String
        System.out.println(method.getResponseBodyAsString());

        //OR as a byte array
        byte [] res  = method.getResponseBody();

        //write to file
        FileOutputStream fos= new FileOutputStream("donepage.html");
        fos.write(res);

        //release connection
        method.releaseConnection();
    }
    catch(IOException e) {
        e.printStackTrace();
    }
  }
}
```

Upon executing this piece of code, you get the following output if the application at the Uniform Resource Locator (URL) you have specified in the code is working properly. Refer to Chapter 4 for details about creating and running validatorStrutsApp, or use the book's source code available in the Downloads section of the Apress Web site (http://www.apress.com/):

```
QueryString>>> firstName=fname&lastName=lname&email=email%40email.com
statusCode>>>200
<html>
<head>
<title>Validation Success Page</title>
<base href="http://localhost:8080/validatorStrutsApp/done.jsp">
</head>
<body bgcolor="white">
<H1>Done! No validation error.<H1>
</body>
</html>
```

The following steps take place in the class SubmitHttpForm to invoke the URL specified, including passing the three parameters as part of the query string, displaying the response, and writing the response to a file:

1. You first need to instantiate the HttpClient, and because you have speci-
    fied no parameters to the constructor, by default the org.apache.
    commons.httpclient.SimpleHttpConnectionManager class is used to create
    a new HttpClient. To use a different ConnectionManager, you can specify
    any class implementing the interface org.apache.commons.httpclient.
    HttpConnectionManager as a parameter to the constructor. You can use the
    MultiThreadedHttpConnectionManager connection manager if more than
    one thread is likely to use the HttpClient. The code would then be new
    HttpClient(new MultiThreadedHttpConnectionManager()).

2. Next you create an instance of HttpMethod. Because HttpClient provides
    implementations for all HTTP methods, you could very well have chosen
    an instance of PostMethod instead of GetMethod. Because you are using an
    HttpMethod reference and not a reference of an implementation class such
    as GetMethod or PostMethod, you intend to use no special features provided
    by implementations such as GetMethod or PostMethod.

3. This is the same example you saw in Chapter 4, so you just have to
    submit an HTML form holding three form fields. For this you define
    name/value pairs and then set an array of those name/value pairs into
    the query string.

4. Once the groundwork is complete, you execute the method using the
    HttpClient instance you created in step 1. The response code returned is
    based on the success or failure of the execution. The response shows
    that the execution was successful, and you get an OK status for the
    HTTP status code 200 that is returned.

5. You get the response body both as a string and as a byte array. The
    response is printed to the console and also written to a file named
    donepage.html.

NOTE *The class* org.apache.commons.httpclient.HttpStatus
defines static int *variables that map to HTTP status codes.*

In this example, you can see how to easily fire a request and get a response
over HTTP using the HttpClient component. You might have noted that writing
such code has a lot of potential to enable testing of Web applications quickly and
to even load test them. This has led to HttpClient being used in popular testing
frameworks such as Jakarta Cactus, HTMLUnit, and so on. You can find in the
documentation a list of popular applications that use HttpClient.

You used the GET method to send name/value pairs as part of a request. However, the GET method cannot always serve your purpose, and in some cases using the POST method is a better option.

Using the POST Method

Listing 9-2 shows an example where you enclose an Extensible Markup Language (XML) file within a request and send it using the POST method to a JSP named GetRequest.jsp. The JSP will just print the request headers it receives. These headers will show if the request got across properly.

Listing 9-2. Sending an XML File Using the POST Method

```
package com.commonsbook.chap9;
import org.apache.commons.httpclient.HttpClient;
import org.apache.commons.httpclient.methods.PostMethod;

import java.io.File;
import java.io.FileInputStream;
import java.io.IOException;

public class PostAFile {
    private static String url =
        "http://localhost:8080/HttpServerSideApp/GetRequest.jsp";

    public static void main(String[] args) throws IOException {
        HttpClient client = new HttpClient();
        PostMethod postMethod = new PostMethod(url);

        client.setConnectionTimeout(8000);

        // Send any XML file as the body of the POST request
        File f = new File("students.xml");
        System.out.println("File Length = " + f.length());

        postMethod.setRequestBody(new FileInputStream(f));
        postMethod.setRequestHeader("Content-type",
            "text/xml; charset=ISO-8859-1");

        int statusCode1 = client.executeMethod(postMethod);

        System.out.println("statusLine>>>" + postMethod.getStatusLine());
        postMethod.releaseConnection();
    }
}
```

In Listing 9-2, I have stated the URL for GetRequest.jsp using a server I am running locally on port 8080. This URL will vary based on the server where the JSP is being maintained. In this example, you create an instance of the classes HttpClient and PostMethod. You set the connection timeout for the HTTP connection to 3,000 milliseconds and then set an XML file into the request body. I am using the same file as used earlier in Chapter 7, Listing 7-2; however, the contents of the file are not relevant to the example, and you could very well use any other file. Because you are sending an XML file, you also set the Content-Type header to state the format and the character set. GetRequest.jsp contains only a scriptlet that prints the request headers. The contents of the GetRequest.jsp file are as follows:

```
<%
        java.util.Enumeration e= request.getHeaderNames();
        while (e.hasMoreElements()) {
          String headerName=(String)e.nextElement();
          System.out.println(headerName +" = "+request.getHeader(headerName));
        }
%>
```

Upon executing the class PostAFile, the JSP gets invoked, and the output displayed on the server console is as follows:

```
content-type = text/xml; charset=ISO-8859-1
user-agent = Jakarta Commons-HttpClient/2.0rc1
host = localhost:8080
content-length = 279
```

The output shown on the console where the PostAFile class was executed is as follows:

```
File Length = 279
statusLine>>>HTTP/1.1 200 OK
```

Note that the output on the server shows the content length as 279 (bytes), the same as the length of the file students.xml that is shown on the application console. Because you are not invoking the JSP using a web browser, the User-Agent header that normally states the browser specifics shows the HttpClient version being used instead.

 NOTE *In this example, you sent a single file over HTTP. To upload multiple files, the* MultipartPostMethod *class is a better alternative. You will look at it later in the "Introducing FileUpload" section.*

Managing Cookies

HttpClient provides cookie management features that can be particularly useful to test the way an application handles cookies. Listing 9-3 shows an example where you use HttpClient to add a cookie to a request and also to list details of cookies set by the JSP you invoke using the HttpClient code.

The HttpState class plays an important role while working with cookies. The HttpState class works as a container for HTTP attributes such as cookies that can persist from one request to another. When you normally surf the Web, the Web browser is what stores the HTTP attributes.

Listing 9-3. CookiesTrial.java

```java
package com.commonsbook.chap9;
import org.apache.commons.httpclient.Cookie;
import org.apache.commons.httpclient.HttpClient;
import org.apache.commons.httpclient.HttpState;
import org.apache.commons.httpclient.cookie.CookiePolicy;
import org.apache.commons.httpclient.methods.GetMethod;

public class CookiesTrial {

    private static String url =
        "http://127.0.0.1:8080/HttpServerSideApp/CookieMgt.jsp";

    public static void main(String[] args) throws Exception {

        //A new cookie for the domain 127.0.0.1
        //Cookie Name= ABCD   Value=00000  Path=/  MaxAge=-1   Secure=False
        Cookie mycookie = new Cookie("127.0.0.1", "ABCD", "00000", "/", -1, false);

        //Create a new HttpState container
        HttpState initialState = new HttpState();
        initialState.addCookie(mycookie);

        //Set to COMPATIBILITY for it to work in as many cases as possible
        initialState.setCookiePolicy(CookiePolicy.COMPATIBILITY);
        //create new client
        HttpClient httpclient = new HttpClient();
        //set the HttpState for the client
        httpclient.setState(initialState);
```

```
GetMethod getMethod = new GetMethod(url);
//Execute a GET method
int result = httpclient.executeMethod(getMethod);

System.out.println("statusLine>>>"+getMethod.getStatusLine());

//Get cookies stored in the HttpState for this instance of HttpClient
Cookie[] cookies = httpclient.getState().getCookies();

for (int i = 0; i < cookies.length; i++) {
    System.out.println("\nCookieName="+cookies[i].getName());
    System.out.println("Value="+cookies[i].getValue());
    System.out.println("Domain="+cookies[i].getDomain());
}

getMethod.releaseConnection();
    }
}
```

In Listing 9-3, you use the HttpState instance to store a new cookie and then associate this instance with the HttpClient instance. You then invoke CookieMgt.jsp. This JSP is meant to print the cookies it finds in the request and then add a cookie of its own. The JSP code is as follows:

```
<%

        Cookie[] cookies= request.getCookies();

        for (int i = 0; i < cookies.length; i++) {
          System.out.println(cookies[i].getName() +" = "+cookies[i].getValue());
        }

        //Add a new cookie
        response.addCookie(new Cookie("XYZ","12345"));
%>
```

 NOTE *HttpClient code uses the class* org.apache.commons. httpclient.Cookie, *and JSP and servlet code uses the class* javax.servlet.http.Cookie.

The output on the application console upon executing the CookiesTrial class and invoking CookieMgt.jsp is as follows:

```
statusLine>>>HTTP/1.1 200 OK

CookieName=ABCD
Value=00000
Domain=127.0.0.1

CookieName=XYZ
Value=12345
Domain=127.0.0.1

CookieName=JSESSIONID
Value=C46581331881A84483F0004390F94508
Domain=127.0.0.1
```

In this output, note that although the cookie named ABCD has been created from CookiesTrial, the other cookie named XYZ is the one inserted by the JSP code. The cookie named JSESSIONID is meant for session tracking and gets created upon invoking the JSP. The output as displayed on the console of the server when the JSP is executed is as follows:

```
ABCD = 00000
```

This shows that when CookieMgt.jsp receives the request from the CookiesTrial class, the cookie named ABCD was the only cookie that existed. The sidebar "HTTPS and Proxy Servers" shows how you should handle requests over HTTPS and configure your client to go through a proxy.

HTTPS and Proxy Servers

Using HttpClient to try out URLs that involve HTTPS is the same as with ordinary URLs. Just state https://... as your URL, and it should work fine. You only need to have Java Secure Socket Extension (JSSE) running properly on your machine. JSSE ships as a part of Java Software Development Kit (JSDK) 1.4 and higher and does not require any separate download and installation.

If you have to go through a proxy server, introduce the following piece of code. Replace PROXYHOST with the host name and replace 9999 with the port number for your proxy server:

```
HttpClient client = new HttpClient();
HostConfiguration hConf= client.getHostConfiguration();
hConf.setProxy("PROXYHOST ", 9999);
```

If you also need to specify a username password for the proxy, you can do this using the setProxyCredentials method of the class HttpState. This method takes a Credentials object as a parameter. Credentials is a marker interface that has no methods and has a single implementation UsernamePasswordCredentials. You can use this class to create a Credentials object that holds the username and password required for Basic authentication.

You will now see the HttpClient component's capability to use MultipartPostMethod to upload multiple files. You will look at this in tandem with the Commons FileUpload component. This Commons component is specifically meant to handle the server-side tasks associated with file uploads.

Introducing FileUpload

The FileUpload component has the capability of simplifying the handling of files uploaded to a server. Note that the FileUpload component is meant for use on the server side; in other words, it handles where the files are being uploaded to—not the client side where the files are uploaded from. Uploading files from an HTML form is pretty simple; however, handling these files when they get to the server is not that simple. If you want to apply any rules and store these files based on those rules, things get more difficult.

The FileUpload component remedies this situation, and in very few lines of code you can easily manage the files uploaded and store them in appropriate locations. You will now see an example where you upload some files first using a standard HTML form and then using HttpClient code.

Using HTML File Upload

The commonly used methodology to upload files is to have an HTML form where you define the files you want to upload. A common example of this HTML interface is the Web page you encounter when you want to attach files to an email while using any of the popular Web mail services.

In this example, you will create a simple HTML page where you provide for three files to be uploaded. Listing 9-4 shows the HTML for this page. Note that the enctype attribute for the form has the value multipart/form-data, and the input tag used is of type file. Based on the value of the action attribute, on form submission, the data is sent to ProcessFileUpload.jsp.

Listing 9-4. `UploadFiles.html`

```
<HTML>
  <HEAD>
    <META HTTP-EQUIV="Content-Type" CONTENT="text/html; charset=windows-1252"/>
    <TITLE>File Upload Page</TITLE>
  </HEAD>
  <BODY>Upload Files
    <FORM name="filesForm" action="ProcessFileUpload.jsp"
    method="post" enctype="multipart/form-data">
        File 1:<input type="file" name="file1"/><br/>
        File 2:<input type="file" name="file2"/><br/>
        File 3:<input type="file" name="file3"/><br/>
        <input type="submit" name="Submit" value="Upload Files"/>
    </FORM>
  </BODY>
</HTML>
```

You can use a servlet to handle the file upload. I have used JSP to minimize the code you need to write. The task that the JSP has to accomplish is to pick up the files that are sent as part of the request and store these files on the server. In the JSP, instead of displaying the result of the upload in the Web browser, I have chosen to print messages on the server console so that you can use this same JSP when it is not invoked through an HTML form but by using HttpClient-based code.

Listing 9-5 shows the JSP code. Note the code that checks whether the item is a form field. This check is required because the Submit button contents are also sent as part of the request, and you want to distinguish between this data and the files that are part of the request. You have set the maximum file size to 1,000,000 bytes using the `setSizeMax` method.

Listing 9-5. `ProcessFileUpload.jsp`

```
<%@ page contentType="text/html;charset=windows-1252"%>
<%@ page import="org.apache.commons.fileupload.DiskFileUpload"%>
<%@ page import="org.apache.commons.fileupload.FileItem"%>
<%@ page import="java.util.List"%>
<%@ page import="java.util.Iterator"%>
<%@ page import="java.io.File"%>
<html>
<head>
<meta http-equiv="Content-Type" content="text/html; charset=windows-1252">
<title>Process File Upload</title>
</head>
```

```
<%
        System.out.println("Content Type ="+request.getContentType());

        DiskFileUpload fu = new DiskFileUpload();
        // If file size exceeds, a FileUploadException will be thrown
        fu.setSizeMax(1000000);

        List fileItems = fu.parseRequest(request);
        Iterator itr = fileItems.iterator();

        while(itr.hasNext()) {
          FileItem fi = (FileItem)itr.next();

          //Check if not form field so as to only handle the file inputs
          //else condition handles the submit button input
          if(!fi.isFormField()) {
            System.out.println("\nNAME: "+fi.getName());
            System.out.println("SIZE: "+fi.getSize());
            //System.out.println(fi.getOutputStream().toString());
            File fNew= new File(application.getRealPath("/"), fi.getName());

            System.out.println(fNew.getAbsolutePath());
            fi.write(fNew);
          }
          else {
            System.out.println("Field ="+fi.getFieldName());
          }
        }
%>
<body>
Upload Successful!!
</body>
</html>
```

CAUTION *With FileUpload 1.0 I found that when the form was submitted using Opera version 7.11, the* getName *method of the class* FileItem *returns just the name of the file. However, if the form is submitted using Internet Explorer 5.5, the filename along with its entire path is returned by the same method. This can cause some problems.*

To run this example, I used the three files you used earlier in Chapter 7. Upon submitting the form using Opera, the output I got on the Tomcat server console was as follows:

```
Content Type =multipart/form-data; boundary=----------rz7ZNYDVpN1To8L73sZ6OE

NAME: academy.xml
SIZE: 951
D:\javaGizmos\jakarta-tomcat-4.0.1\webapps\HttpServerSideApp\academy.xml

NAME: academyRules.xml
SIZE: 1211
D:\javaGizmos\jakarta-tomcat-4.0.1\webapps\HttpServerSideApp\academyRules.xml

NAME: students.xml
SIZE: 279
D:\javaGizmos\jakarta-tomcat-4.0.1\webapps\HttpServerSideApp\students.xml
Field =Submit
```

However, when submitting this same form using Internet Explorer 5.5, the output on the server console was as follows:

```
Content Type =multipart/form-data; boundary=-------------------------7d3bb1de0
2e4

NAME: D:\temp\academy.xml
SIZE: 951
D:\javaGizmos\jakarta-tomcat-4.0.1\webapps\HttpServerSideApp\D:\temp\academy.xml
```

The browser displayed the following message: "The requested resource (D:\javaGizmos\jakarta-tomcat-4.0.1\webapps\HttpServerSideApp\D:\temp\academy.xml (The filename, directory name, or volume label syntax is incorrect)) is not available."

This contrasting behavior on different browsers can cause problems. One workaround that I found in an article at http://www.onjava.com/pub/a/onjava/2003/06/25/commons.html is to first create a file reference with whatever is supplied by the getName method and then create a new file reference using the name returned by the earlier file reference. Therefore, you can insert the following code to have your code work with both browsers (I wonder who the guilty party is . . . blaming Microsoft is always the easy way out):

```
File tempFileRef = new File(fi.getName());
File fNew = new File(application.getRealPath("/"),tempFileRef.getName());
```

In this section, you uploaded files using a standard HTML form mechanism. However, often a need arises to be able to upload files from within your Java code, without any browser or form coming into the picture. In the next section, you will look at HttpClient-based file upload.

Using HttpClient-Based FileUpload

Earlier in the chapter you saw some of the capabilities of the HttpClient component. One capability I did not cover was its ability to send multipart requests. In this section, you will use this capability to upload a few files to the same JSP that you used for uploads using HTML.

The class org.apache.commons.httpclient.methods.MultipartPostMethod provides the multipart method capability to send multipart-encoded forms, and the package org.apache.commons.httpclient.methods.multipart has the support classes required. Sending a multipart form using HttpClient is quite simple. In the code in Listing 9-6, you send three files to ProcessFileUpload.jsp.

Listing 9-6. HttpMultiPartFileUpload.java

```java
package com.commonsbook.chap9;
import java.io.File;
import java.io.IOException;

import org.apache.commons.httpclient.HttpClient;
import org.apache.commons.httpclient.methods.MultipartPostMethod;

public class HttpMultiPartFileUpload {
    private static String url =
      "http://localhost:8080/HttpServerSideApp/ProcessFileUpload.jsp";

    public static void main(String[] args) throws IOException {
        HttpClient client = new HttpClient();
        MultipartPostMethod mPost = new MultipartPostMethod(url);
        client.setConnectionTimeout(8000);

        // Send any XML file as the body of the POST request
        File f1 = new File("students.xml");
        File f2 = new File("academy.xml");
        File f3 = new File("academyRules.xml");

        System.out.println("File1 Length = " + f1.length());
        System.out.println("File2 Length = " + f2.length());
        System.out.println("File3 Length = " + f3.length());

        mPost.addParameter(f1.getName(), f1);
        mPost.addParameter(f2.getName(), f2);
        mPost.addParameter(f3.getName(), f3);
```

```
                int statusCode1 = client.executeMethod(mPost);

                System.out.println("statusLine>>>" + mPost.getStatusLine());
                mPost.releaseConnection();
        }
}
```

In this code, you just add the files as parameters and execute the method. The `ProcessFileUpload.jsp` file gets invoked, and the output is as follows:

```
Content Type =multipart/form-data; boundary=----------------31415926535897932384
6

NAME: students.xml
SIZE: 279
D:\javaGizmos\jakarta-tomcat-4.0.1\webapps\HttpServerSideApp\students.xml

NAME: academy.xml
SIZE: 951
D:\javaGizmos\jakarta-tomcat-4.0.1\webapps\HttpServerSideApp\academy.xml

NAME: academyRules.xml
SIZE: 1211
D:\javaGizmos\jakarta-tomcat-4.0.1\webapps\HttpServerSideApp\academyRules.xml
```

Thus, file uploads on the server side become quite a simple task if you are using the Commons FileUpload component.

Summary

In this chapter, you saw the HttpClient and FileUpload components. Although HttpClient can be useful in any kind of applications that use HTTP for communication, the FileUpload component has a much more specific scope. One important plus for HttpClient is the existence of a decent user guide and tutorial. The FileUpload component can be just what you are looking for if you are wondering what to use and how to manage files uploaded through your application.

CHAPTER 10

Using the Net
Component

THE COMMONS NET COMPONENT provides classes that make using various protocols such as Telnet, Post Office Protocol 3 (POP3), File Transfer Protocol (FTP),
Network News Transfer Protocol (NNTP), Simple Mail Transfer Protocol (SMTP),
and so on easier. The rationale for the project has been nicely stated on the Web
site as follows: "Java doesn't provide an API for common Internet protocols. Many
applications need to communicate via well-known Internet protocols such as
FTP, SMTP, and Telnet." In this chapter, you will explore the Net component's
capabilities with regard to commonly used protocols, and you will see examples
that demonstrate how to use the component. Table 10-1 shows the component
details.

Table 10-1. Component Details

Name	Version	Package
Net	1.1.0	org.apache.commons.net

Introducing the Net Component

The component has its origins in a commercial product named NetComponents.
Once the contract obligations for NetComponents expired, the code was made
available under the Apache license. The creators emphasize on the project's Web
page that "The purpose of the library is to provide fundamental protocol access,
not higher-level abstractions." Although the component is capable of providing
fundamental protocol access, for most users advanced protocol capabilities are
not required. Being able to easily manage basic protocol tasks is a requirement
that is more frequently encountered than having to work with core protocol issues.
I say this because generally the requirement will be something such as sending
mail where the functionality is important and the protocol is incidental. As
long as the mail gets sent, the developer might not care much about protocol
technicalities.

In this chapter, you will encounter many references to Transmission Control Protocol (TCP) and User Datagram Protocol (UDP), which are transport layer networking protocols that sit on top of the Internet Protocol (IP). TCP is integral to the Internet and is something that all of us use every day. UDP is a little different and works by sending datagrams across the network. A *datagram* is a unit of binary data. The Computer Networking section at http://compnetworking.about.com/ is a good place to look up definitions and some of the basics of networking.

With regard to how the Net component is built, you will find that all client classes for specific protocols extend either the SocketClient or DatagramSocketClient class:

SocketClient: The SocketClient class provides basic operations required for client objects using sockets. So the protocol-specific client classes do not have to rewrite socket-handling code. You can define the Factory that the SocketClient will use to create a specific type of socket. For this the interface SocketFactory needs to be implemented by the Factory to be used. An instance of the Factory can then be provided to the SocketClient using the setSocketFactory method of the SocketClient class. SMTP, NNTP, POP3 and a few other classes extend the SocketClient class.

DatagramSocketClient: The DatagramSocketClient class provides basic operations required of client objects using datagram sockets. To define the Factory that the DatagramSocketClient will use to create new datagram sockets, the interface DatagramSocketFactory needs to be implemented by the Factory to be used. A Factory class instance can then be provided to the specific DatagramSocketClient using the setDatagramSocketFactory method of the class DatagramSocketClient.

NOTE   *A* Factory *is a design pattern concept that is used to isolate and control the creation of objects. The Factory Method and Abstract Factory are popular design patterns. Most books on design patterns will discuss what a* Factory *is.*

The Net component supports the protocols listed in Table 10-2 and provides client classes that simplify the protocol usage. Although separate packages exist for some protocols such as SMTP, POP, and so on, the other client classes are located in the org.apache.commons.net package.

Table 10-2. Protocol and Client Class

Protocol	Client Class	Description	Request for Comments (RFC)
SMTP	`org.apache.commons.net.smtp.SMTPClient`	Send email using SMTP	821
POP3	`org.apache.commons.net.pop3.POP3Client`	Use POP for fetching emails	1939
FTP	`org.apache.commons.net.ftp.FTPClient`	Store and retrieve files using FTP	959
NNTP	`org.apache.commons.net.nntp.NNTPClient`	Post and retrieve articles from newsgroups using NNTP	977
Telnet	`org.apache.commons.net.telnet.TelnetClient`	Implements the simple Network Virtual Terminal (NVT) for the Telnet protocol	854
TFTP	`org.apache.commons.net.tftp.TFTPClient`	Receive and send files using Trivial File Transfer Protocol (TFTP)	783
Character generator protocol	`org.apache.commons.net.CharGenTCPClient and org.apache.commons.net.CharGenUDPClient`	TCP and UDP implementation for the Character generator protocol	864
Daytime	`org.apache.commons.net.DaytimeTCPClient and org.apache.commons.net.DaytimeUDPClient`	TCP and UDP implementation for the Daytime protocol	867
Discard	`org.apache.commons.net.DiscardTCPClient and org.apache.commons.net.DiscardUDPClient`	TCP and UDP implementation for the Discard protocol	863
Echo	`org.apache.commons.net.EchoTCPClient and org.apache.commons.net.EchoUDPClient`	TCP and UDP implementation for the Echo protocol	862
Finger	`org.apache.commons.net.FingerClient`	Implementation of a client for Internet Finger protocol	1288
Time	`org.apache.commons.net.TimeTCPClient and org.apache.commons.net.TimeUDPClient`	TCP and UDP implementation of client for Time protocol	868
Whois	`org.apache.commons.net.WhoisClient`	Implementation of Whois client	954

For more information about all the Request for Comments (RFCs) referred to in Table 10-2, check out http://www.faqs.org/rfcs/rfcxxxx.html where xxxx stands for the RFC number. Another resource is http://www.ietf.org/rfc.html, which can get you more information about the various RFCs. The RFC index at http://www.ietf.org/iesg/1rfc_index.txt lists all RFCs in numeric order. Note the dates for the protocols. RFC 821 for SMTP that millions of people use everyday is dated August 1982!

You can download the Commons Net component from http://jakarta. apache.org/commons/net/. I will now cover some of the protocols that the Net component supports, beginning with the SMTP, which is used to send emails.

Working with Simple Mail Transfer Protocol (SMTP)

Automatically sending emails from the application is a requirement present in a large number of today's applications. The Net component provides good support for SMTP that can get you sending mails in very few lines of code. Java does provide a standard JavaMail Application Programming Interface (API) that is meant specifically for working with emails and, because it is a standard, is a better choice than the Net component in many cases. However, sending mails and handling protocol-specific tasks using the Net component is just as simple as with the JavaMail API. You will see the Net component's emailing capabilities in this chapter, but you should also explore the JavaMail API before you decide which to use.

The package org.apache.commons.net.smtp contains the classes that provide the SMTP functionality. The class SMTP in this package provides the basic functionality for SMTP. However, the user is expected to use the SMTPClient class that is a subclass of SMTP class. The SMTPClient abstracts low-level details of SMTP from the user and provides a higher-level interface. To use the SMTPClient, you need no more understanding of SMTP than what you would require to configure and send mails from your email software.

 TIP *Throughout the Net component, for all protocol clients derived from class* SocketClient, *the approach is generally to instantiate a* Client *class provided in the package, connect to the server, perform an action, and disconnect.*

Apart from the SMTPClient, another class you need to use is the SimpleSMTPHeader. An instance of SimpleSMTPHeader provides the header details required while sending

an email message using SMTP. Listing 10-1 shows an example so you can understand the code involved.

Listing 10-1. SMTPClientTrial

```
package com.commonsbook.chap10;
import org.apache.commons.net.smtp.SMTPClient;
import org.apache.commons.net.smtp.SMTPReply;
import org.apache.commons.net.smtp.SimpleSMTPHeader;

import java.io.IOException;
import java.io.Writer;

public final class SMTPClientTrial {
    public static void main(String[] args) {
        sendmail("smtp.example.com", "sender@example.com",
            "recipient@example.com", "ccrecipient@example.com",
            "Message Subject", "A Test message");
    }

    private static void sendmail(String smtpServer, String senderMail,
        String recipientMail, String ccrecipient, String subject,
        String message) {
        SMTPClient client = null;

        try {
            //Create new SMTPClient instance
            client = new SMTPClient();

            // Use the SimpleSMTPHeader class to generate a minimum SMTP header
            SimpleSMTPHeader header = new SimpleSMTPHeader(senderMail,
                    recipientMail, subject);

            //connect to server
            client.connect(smtpServer);

            //Print string retruend by server
            System.out.print(client.getReplyString());

            //Check Reply Code from server.
            //All codes beginning with a 2 are positive completion responses
            if (!SMTPReply.isPositiveCompletion(client.getReplyCode())) {
                client.disconnect();
```

```
            System.out.println("Connection Refused");
            System.exit(1);
        }

        //login
        client.login();

        //Set Sender for the mail
        client.setSender(senderMail);

        //Add recepient
        client.addRecipient(recipientMail);

        if ((ccrecipient != null) || !"".equals(ccrecipient)) {
            client.addRecipient(ccrecipient);
            header.addCC(ccrecipient);
        }

        //Sends SMTP DATA command in preparation to send an email message.
        //Returns the writer to which the mesage is written.
        Writer writer = client.sendMessageData();

        if (writer != null) {
            //Write SMTP Header
            writer.write(header.toString());
            writer.write(message);
            writer.close();

            //finalize the transaction and verify its success
            //or failure from the server reply.
            boolean completion = client.completePendingCommand();

            if (completion) {
                System.out.println("Mail sent successfully");
            }
        }

        client.logout();
        client.disconnect();
    } catch (IOException e) {
        if (client.isConnected()) {
            try {
                client.disconnect();
```

```
        } catch (IOException f) {
            // ignore
        }
    }

    e.printStackTrace();
}
    }
}
```

SMTPClientTrial as shown in Listing 10-1 is a class that, upon execution, will send a message from sender@example.com to recipient@example.com with the subject "Message Subject" and the message "A Test Message." You call the method sendmail from the main method, providing all the parameters that are essential for sending an email using SMTP. You can provide appropriate parameters and reuse the sendmail method in your code.

NOTE *The default port that the* SMTPClient *uses for communication with the SMTP server is 25. If your provider uses a different port, you can configure that using the* setDefaultPort *method provided. If your SMTP server requires authentication, as of version 1.1.0, that cannot be done using the* SMTPClient.

The steps involved in sending a mail in the method sendmail in Listing 10-1 are as follows:

1. Create a new instance of SMTPClient.

2. Create a new instance of SimpleSMTPHeader. This class can create an SMTP header that will be good enough for most usages. For more complex headers, you can create and use a different SMTP header class.

3. Connect to the SMTP server.

4. Check whether the reply is a positive completion response. All codes beginning with a 2 are positive completion responses.

5. Log in to the server. Note that connecting and logging in are distinct tasks, and you need to connect before you log in.

6. Set the sender and the recipient for the mail.

7. Check if a recipient for the Carbon Copy (CC) of the mail exists. If there is one, add to the header using the method addCC and to the client using the addRecipient method. You use the addRecipient method of the SMTPClient class irrespective of it being a To email address or a CC one. So the addCC method of the SimpleSMTPHeader is what distinguishes between a To address and a CC one.

8. Invoke the sendMessageData method. This is an important step that sends the SMTP DATA command in preparation to send an email message. The call returns a Writer instance in which you can write the header and contents of the mail. The Writer instance is of type org.apache.commons.net.io.DotTerminatedMessageWriter. Note that until you close the Writer, no fresh commands should be issued to the SMTP server.

9. Write the header and message to the Writer instance and then close the writer.

10. Invoke the completePendingCommand method to finalize the transaction. The returned value true/false tells you if the mail was sent successfully.

11. Log out and disconnect.

Some other useful methods provided by the class SMTPClient are as follows:

- **boolean sendShortMessageData(String message)**: This method gets the Writer, writes the message, and also calls the completePendingCommand method. In turn, you are eliminating a couple of steps from the listing earlier.

- **boolean sendSimpleMessage(String sender, String recipient, String message)**: This method is a utility method that you can use to quickly send an email to a single recipient. This method internally uses the sendShortMessageData method.

- **boolean sendSimpleMessage(String sender, String[] recipients, String message)**: This sends a message to multiple recipients.

- **String listHelp()**: This fetches help from the server.

- **String listHelp(String command)**: This fetches help for a specific command.

- **boolean sendNoOp()**: This prevents server timeouts by sending the NOOP command to the server.

Now that you have seen how you can quite easily send emails from any Java application, you will look at another popular email protocol, POP3.

Working with Post Office Protocol 3 (POP3)

In the earlier section you saw how you could send emails using the SMTP capabilities of the Net component. Now you will see how you can check your mail using the Net component and POP3. POP3 is a popular protocol that is used by many mail providers to let users check their email using any POP3 client. Internet Message Access Protocol (IMAP) is a newer protocol that is also used by some providers. Check your email provider's Web site to see which protocol is being used. The Net component as yet does not provide IMAP capabilities; however, JavaMail does support IMAP. The Web site http://www.emailaddresses.com/ is a good resource to check out which mail providers provide the POP3 facility. POP3 capability used to be free until a couple of years back but now most of the top email providers, such as Yahoo, charge for the service.

If your email provider does support POP3, the configuration information you need to access mail from your Java code is just the name of the POP3 server, your username, and password.

The POP3 classes are located in the package org.apache.commons.net.pop3. The class POP3Client is the class you will be using the most. POP3Client extends the class POP3 that provides a lot of protocol-specific functionality. If you want to write and use your own client class instead of the class POP3Client provided, extending class POP3 is the way to go about it.

NOTE *The default port that the* POP3Client *uses for communication with the POP3 server is 110. If your provider uses a different port, you can configure it by using the* setDefaultPort *method provided.*

Listing 10-2 shows an example where you check mail from a server that supports POP3.

Listing 10-2. POP3ClientTrial

```
package com.commonsbook.chap10;
import org.apache.commons.net.io.*;
import org.apache.commons.net.pop3.*;

import java.io.*;
```

```java
public class POP3ClientTrial {
    public static void main(String[] args) {
        listMails("pop. example.com", "username", "password");
    }

    public static void listMails(String popserver, String username,
        String password) {
        POP3Client client = null;

        try {
            client = new POP3Client();
            System.out.println("Port >>" + client.getDefaultPort());
            client.connect(popserver);

            if (client.getState() != POP3.AUTHORIZATION_STATE) {
                System.out.println("Unable to connect to POP server");
                return;
            }

            if (!client.login(username, password)) {
                System.out.println("Unable to login to POP server");
                return;
            }

            POP3MessageInfo[] pop3Messages = client.listMessages();

            if (pop3Messages != null) {
                for (int i = 0; i < pop3Messages.length; i++) {
                    POP3MessageInfo message = pop3Messages[i];
                    System.out.println("***Identifier >>" + message.identifier);
                    System.out.println("***Number >>" + message.number);
                    System.out.println("***Size >>" + message.size);

                    Reader reader = client.retrieveMessage(message.number);
                    System.out.println(reader);

                    if (reader != null) {
                        BufferedReader bufReader = new BufferedReader(reader);
                        String line;

                        while ((line = bufReader.readLine()) != null) {
                            System.out.println(line);
                        }
                    }
                }
```

```
            }
        }

        client.logout();
        client.disconnect();
    } catch (IOException e) {
        if (client.isConnected()) {
            try {
                client.disconnect();
            } catch (IOException f) {
                // ignore
            }
        }

        e.printStackTrace();
    }
    }
}
```

In this example, the method listMails does all the work and can be easily reused. The steps involved in the working of the method listMails are as follows:

1. Instantiate POP3Client, and connect to the server.

2. Because the connect method return type is void, you have to check the client state using the method getState. If the client is not in AUTHORIZATION_STATE, you print an error message and exit.

3. Log in to the server. Note that, like the SMTP client, connect and login are separate tasks that need to be performed in this order.

4. Use the listMessages method to get an array of POP3MessageInfo instances. The POP3MessageInfo class has three fields: identifier, number, and size. In case of the listMessages method, the identifier field value will always be null. The number field contains the message number, and size contains the message size.

5. Iterate through the POP3MessageInfo array. For each message, use the message number to get the Reader for that message. The Reader is of type org.apache.commons.net.io.DotTerminatedMessageReader.

6. Use a java.io.BufferedReader to read the contents from the Reader for each message.

The `POP3MessageInfo` class plays an important role in `POP3Client` usage because most data returned by methods in the `POP3Client` is in the form of objects of `POP3MessageInfo`. The POP3Client class provides some other methods that can come in handy. These methods are as follows:

- **boolean deleteMessage(int messageId)**: This deletes the message whose message number is provided.

- **boolean noop()**: This sends a `NOOP` command to prevent the connection from timing out. Note that the method name in the case of `POP3Client` is noop, and in other cases such as `SMTPClient` and `FTPClient`, the name of a method performing the same function is sendNoOp.

- **POP3MessageInfo status()**: This gets the status of the mailbox. The number property in the `POP3MessageInfo` instance returned holds the value of the number of messages present. The size property holds the combined size of all messages present on the server.

- **java.io.Reader retrieveMessageTop(int messageId, int numLines)**: This retrieves only a specified number of lines from the message.

Now that you know how to check mail using POP3, you will move on to the FTP capabilities of the Net component.

Working with File Transfer Protocol (FTP)

The classes handling the FTP capabilities of the Net component are located in the package `org.apache.commons.net.ftp`. The class `org.apache.commons.net.ftp.FTPClient` is an FTP client that is provided by the component and should be able to handle most of your FTP requirements.

Like the `SMTPClient` and `POP3Client` classes you saw in earlier sections, `FTPClient` also extends the `org.apache.commons.net.SocketClient`, so some of the steps involved in using `FTPClient` are similar to `SMTPClient` and `POP3Client`. Listing 10-3 shows an example.

Listing 10-3. `FTPClientTrial`

```
package com.commonsbook.chap10;
import org.apache.commons.net.ftp.*;

import java.io.*;
```

```java
public class FTPClientTrial {
    public static void main(String[] args) {
        new FTPClientTrial().useFTP("ftp. example.com", "/directory", "file",
            "username", "password");
    }

    public void useFTP(String ftpserver, String directoryName,
        String filetoUpload, String username, String password) {
        FTPClient ftpClient = new FTPClient();

        try {
            ftpClient.connect(ftpserver);
            System.out.print(ftpClient.getReplyString());

            // check reply code.
            if (!FTPReply.isPositiveCompletion(ftpClient.getReplyCode())) {
                ftpClient.disconnect();
                System.out.println("Connection refused.");
                return;
            }

            ftpClient.login(username, password);
            System.out.println("Workdir >>" +
                ftpClient.printWorkingDirectory());
            ftpClient.changeWorkingDirectory(directoryName);

            //Store file
            FileInputStream input = new FileInputStream(filetoUpload);
            ftpClient.storeFile(filetoUpload, input);

            //List all Files and directories
            FTPFile[] files = ftpClient.listFiles();

            if (files != null) {
                for (int i = 0; i < files.length; i++) {
                    //If file print name and size
                    if (files[i].isFile()) {
                        System.out.println("File >> " + files[i].getName() +
                            "\tSize >>" + files[i].getSize());
                    }
                }
            }
```

```
            ftpClient.logout();
            ftpClient.disconnect();
        } catch (IOException e) {
            if (ftpClient.isConnected()) {
                try {
                    ftpClient.disconnect();
                } catch (IOException f) {
                    // do nothing
                }
            }

            e.printStackTrace();
        }
    }
}
```

In Listing 10-3, the method useFTP is where the action is. The steps involved in how the useFTP method works are as follows: Steps 1 through 6 take care of connecting to the server and uploading a file, and steps 7 and 8 do the downloading. To download files from an FTP server without uploading any, just comment out the code for steps 5 and 6:

1. Instantiate FTPClient, and connect to the FTP server using the connect method.

2. Check the reply code using the isPositiveCompletion method of the FTPReply class. All codes beginning with 2 denote a positive completion. The FTPReply class defines many reply code constants and also provides methods such as isPositiveCompletion to check the reply codes.

3. Log in to the FTP server.

4. Print the working directory and then change the working directory to the directory specified.

5. Next you open a FileInputStream to the file you intend to store on the FTP server in the working directory.

6. Use the storeFile method to store the file on the server, using the filename and the FileInputStream specified.

7. Once you are done storing the file, list all the files in the current directory using the `listFiles` method. The class `org.apache.commons.net.ftp.DefaultFTPFileListParser` is used by default as the parser for the files listing. For special cases, you can write a new file list parser by writing a class that implements the `FTPFileListParser` interface.

8. Next iterate through the array of `FTPFile` instances and when a file is found, print the filename and the size of the file. You can check directories using the `isDirectory` method of the `FTPFile` class.

Thus, in a few lines of code, you can get details of files in a directory on an FTP server and even store a new file in that directory. The following are some other useful methods of the `FTPClient` class:

- **boolean appendFile(String filenameOnServer, InputStream local)**: This appends to a file on the server the input from the specified `InputStream`.

- **OutputStream appendFileStream(String filenameOnServer)**: This gets an `OutputStream` to the specified file on the server. Content can be appended to the file using this `OutputStream`.

- **boolean changeToParentDirectory()**: This changes to the parent directory of the current working directory.

- **FTPFileList createFileList(String pathname, FTPFileEntryParser parser)**: This uses a developer-specified implementation of the `FTPFileEntryParser` interface to generate a `FTPFileList` holding information of a file or directory. The abstract class `org.apache.commons.net.ftp.FTPFileListParserImpl` is an implementation of the `FTPFileEntryParser` interface that is provided in the package.

- **boolean deleteFile(java.lang.String pathname)**: This deletes the specified file.

- **String getStatus(java.lang.String pathname)**: This gets the status for the path specified.

- **String[] listNames()**: This gets a list of files in the current working directory.

- **boolean makeDirectory(java.lang.String pathname)**: This creates a new directory in the current working directory if the path specified is a relative path; in the case of an absolute path, this creates a directory at the location specified.

- **boolean removeDirectory(java.lang.String pathname)**: This removes a directory. The directory needs to be empty.

- **boolean rename(java.lang.String from, java.lang.String to)**: This renames a file.

- **boolean sendNoOp()**: This sends a NOOP command to avoid timeout.

These are some other methods provided by the FTPClient that make it quite a powerful tool to work with FTP. You will now look at the NNTP capabilities of the Net component.

Working with Network News Transfer Protocol (NNTP)

NNTP specifies a protocol for distributing, inquiring, retrieving, and posting news articles. Currently thousands of newsgroups on varied topics exist and are hosted by NNTP servers. Although you can easily access these newsgroups using special client software or even some of the more popular email clients, accessing them through Java code can be a little difficult. Using the Net component, you can quite easily perform various tasks associated with newsgroups, such as retrieving a list of newsgroups, articles, posting to newsgroups, and so on.

The package org.apache.commons.net.nntp holds the NNTP classes of the Net component. The class org.apache.commons.net.nntp.NNTP is where the NNTP-specific code is written. However, the user is expected to use its subclass, the NNTPClient class.

You can find a list of free NNTP servers at http://www.free-newsservers.com/free_list1.asp. The steps involved are similar to the SMTP and POP3 examples you saw earlier. The methods of NNTPClient you will find useful are as follows:

- **listNewsgroups**: This lists all newsgroups on the NNTP server.

- **selectNewsgroup**: This method selects a newsgroup. You can then retrieve articles from this newsgroup or post new articles to it.

- **retrieveArticle**: This retrieves article from selected newsgroup.

- **retrieveArticleHeader**: This returns article headers.

- **retrieveArticleBody**: This retrieves article body.

- **postArticle**: This posts a new article.

Listing 10-4 is an example where you search for newsgroups based on a keyword. You then pick up the first newsgroup from the list that the search returns and display the details of the first article in that list.

Listing 10-4. NNTPClientTrial *Class*

```
package com.commonsbook.chap10;
import org.apache.commons.net.nntp.NNTPClient;
import org.apache.commons.net.nntp.NNTPReply;
import org.apache.commons.net.nntp.NewsgroupInfo;

import java.io.BufferedReader;
import java.io.IOException;
import java.io.Reader;

public class NNTPClientTrial {
    public static void main(String[] args) {
        listNewsgroups("freenews.netfront.net", "marathi");
    }

    public static void listNewsgroups(String servername, String keyword) {
        NNTPClient nntpClient = new NNTPClient();
        NewsgroupInfo[] list;

        try {
            nntpClient = new NNTPClient();
            nntpClient.connect(servername);

            // check reply code.
            if (!NNTPReply.isPositiveCompletion(nntpClient.getReplyCode())) {
                nntpClient.disconnect();
                System.out.println("Connection refused.");
                System.exit(1);
            }

            list = nntpClient.listNewsgroups("*" + keyword + "*");

            if ((list != null) && (list.length > 0)) {
                String newsgroup = list[0].getNewsgroup();
                System.out.println("Newsgroup >>" + newsgroup);
                System.out.println("Count >>" + list[0].getArticleCount());
```

```
                    //Select Newsgroup
                    NewsgroupInfo selectedGroupInfo = new NewsgroupInfo();
                    nntpClient.selectNewsgroup(newsgroup, selectedGroupInfo);

                    int iFirstArticle = selectedGroupInfo.getFirstArticle();
                    int iLastArticle = selectedGroupInfo.getLastArticle();

                    System.out.println("First Article >>" + iFirstArticle);
                    System.out.println("Last Article >>" + iLastArticle);

                    //Retrieve Article
                    System.out.println("**ARTICLE**");
                    printFromReader(nntpClient.retrieveArticle(iFirstArticle));

                    //Retrieve Article Info
                    System.out.println("**ARTICLE INFO**");
                    printFromReader(nntpClient.retrieveArticleInfo(iFirstArticle));

                    //Retrieve Article Body
                    System.out.println("**ARTICLE BODY**");
                    printFromReader(nntpClient.retrieveArticleBody(iFirstArticle));

                    //Retrieve Article Header
                    System.out.println("**ARTICLE HEADER**");
                    printFromReader(nntpClient.retrieveArticleHeader(iFirstArticle));
                }

            nntpClient.logout();
            nntpClient.disconnect();
        } catch (IOException e) {
            if (nntpClient.isConnected()) {
                try {
                    nntpClient.disconnect();
                } catch (IOException f) {
                    // do nothing
                }
            }

            e.printStackTrace();
        }
    }
```

```
    private static void printFromReader(Reader reader)
        throws IOException {
        if (reader != null) {
            BufferedReader bufReader = new BufferedReader(reader);
            String line;

            while ((line = bufReader.readLine()) != null) {
                System.out.println(line);
            }

            reader.close();
        }
    }
}
```

Upon executing this code, the group name, article count, and details of the first article will be displayed. Note the use of the method selectNewsgroup followed by picking the count for the first article and the last article. Do not expect the article count to begin with 0 or 1, or any definite number for that matter. It varies across newsgroups, and even the first article count can be a pretty big number.

As listed in Table 10-1, the Net component supports many other protocols besides SMTP, POP, FTP, and NNTP. You will now look at the Net component's capabilities with respect to some of these other protocols.

Working with Time and Daytime

As yet you have seen only clients that used the SocketClient class for communication. You will now learn how you can use the DatagramSocketClient class to communicate using the Time protocol. You can use the org.apache.commons.net. TimeUDPClient and org.apache.commons.net.TimeTCPClient classes for communicating using the Time protocol. The Time protocol is one of the simplest ones around; the RFC says this: "This protocol provides a site-independent, machine-readable date and time. The Time service sends back to the originating source the time in seconds since midnight on January 1, 1900."

 NOTE *Time and Daytime will return the time and date at the server and not at the client. So unless you are hitting a server in your time zone, you could get a different date and time.*

The class TimeUDPClient is what you will look at first. Because this class extends DatagramSocketClient, the steps involved in its usage are unlike any of the examples you have seen so far.

NOTE *For trying out the Time and Daytime protocols, you need to find servers that support these protocols. I found a list of such servers at http://www.kloth.net/software/timesrv1.php. Of those listed, I am using the gnomon.cc.columbia.edu server for the Time and Daytime examples that follow.*

Communicating using UDP is actually easier than the earlier examples because you do not need to connect to or disconnect from servers. You simply need to open a datagram socket, send a datagram, and receive a datagram in response. Listing 10-5 shows an example of using the TimeUDPClient.

Listing 10-5. TimeUDPClientTrial

```
package com.commonsbook.chap10;
import org.apache.commons.net.TimeUDPClient;

import java.net.InetAddress;

import java.util.Date;

public class TimeUDPClientTrial {
    public static void main(String[] args) throws Exception {
        printDateTime("gnomon.cc.columbia.edu");
    }

    public static void printDateTime(String host) throws Exception {
        TimeUDPClient client = new TimeUDPClient();

        //set timeout
        client.setDefaultTimeout(30000);

        //open socket
        client.open();

        //Get time in seconds
        System.out.println("Time >>" +
            client.getTime(InetAddress.getByName(host)));

        //Get java.util.Date
        System.out.println("Date >>" +
            client.getDate(InetAddress.getByName(host)));
        client.close();
    }
}
```

If you want to communicate using TCP instead of UDP for the Time protocol, the client class to be used is TimeTCPClient (see Listing 10-6).

Listing 10-6. TimeTCPClientTrial

```
package com.commonsbook.chap10;
import org.apache.commons.net.TimeTCPClient;

import java.net.InetAddress;

import java.util.Date;

public class TimeTCPClientTrial {
    public static void main(String[] args) throws Exception {
        printDateTime("gnomon.cc.columbia.edu");
    }

    public static void printDateTime(String host) throws Exception {
        TimeTCPClient client = new TimeTCPClient();

        // set timeout
        client.setDefaultTimeout(30000);
        client.connect(host);

        //Get Time in seconds
        System.out.println("Time >>" + client.getTime());

        client.connect(host);

        //Get java.util.Date
        System.out.println("Date >>" + client.getDate());

        client.disconnect();
    }
}
```

Note that in the case of TimeTCPClient, you have to call the connect method again before you call the getDate method. This needs to be done because after the call to getTime the server closes the connection, so you need to connect afresh before you call the method getDate. The code does not work if you miss this step. The output upon execution of Listing 10-5 and Listing 10-6 is similar to this:

```
Time >>3283355131
Date >>Sun Jan 18 00:35:32 GMT+05:30 2004
```

The Daytime protocol is another simple protocol that returns time. You again have the option of using TCP or UDP. The DaytimeUDPClient and DaytimeTCPClient classes use port 13. The gnomon.cc.columbia.edu server you used for the Time examples in Listing 10-5 and 10-6 also provides Daytime protocol support over port 13. Listing 10-7 shows an example of using DaytimeUDPClient.

Listing 10-7. DaytimeUDPClientTrial

```
package com.commonsbook.chap10;
import org.apache.commons.net.DaytimeUDPClient;

import java.net.InetAddress;

public class DaytimeUDPClientTrial {
    public static void main(String[] args) throws Exception {
        System.out.println("DayTime >>" + getDayTime("gnomon.cc.columbia.edu"));
    }

    public static String getDayTime(String host) throws Exception {
        DaytimeUDPClient client = new DaytimeUDPClient();

        // set timeout
        client.setDefaultTimeout(30000);
        client.open();

        //Get Time
        String dayTime = client.getTime(InetAddress.getByName(host)).trim();
        client.close();

        return dayTime;
    }
}
```

Listing 10-8 shows how you can use DaytimeTCPClient to get the time using TCP instead of UDP. Note that once the call to getTime is done, the server will have closed the connection; therefore, if you want to again call the getTime method, you will have to call the connect method again.

Listing 10-8. DaytimeTCPClientTrial

```
package com.commonsbook.chap10;
import org.apache.commons.net.*;
```

```
public class DaytimeTCPClientTrial {
    public static void main(String[] args) throws Exception {
        System.out.println("DayTime >>" + getDayTime("gnomon.cc.columbia.edu"));
    }

    public static String getDayTime(String host) throws Exception {
        DaytimeTCPClient client = new DaytimeTCPClient();

        // set timeout
        client.setDefaultTimeout(30000);
        client.connect(host);

        String dayTime = client.getTime().trim();
        client.disconnect();

        return dayTime;
    }
}
```

The output upon executing both examples of using the Daytime protocol
will be similar to this:

```
DayTime >>Sat Jan 17 19:05:15 2004
```

You now have used many of the protocols that the Net component supports.
If you have no choice and you just have to stick with the java.net package, looking at the source code for the various clients in the Net component can certainly
simplify your task.

Summary

In this chapter, you looked at the Net component, which can be quite useful if
you are working with various protocols. You also saw examples for SMTP, POP,
FTP, Time, and Daytime protocols. Table 10-1 lists all the protocols supported
and the corresponding client classes and the RFCs to which to refer.

Although the Net component can serve as an abstraction over the protocol
technicalities, it is quite capable of doing in-depth and protocol-specific tasks. In
the next chapter, you will see some more really cool components.

CHAPTER 11

Using Other Commons Components

IN THIS CHAPTER, you will look at some Commons components that are quite useful and that also hold promise for the future. I will briefly cover each component and try to demonstrate its capabilities using examples. Table 11-1 gives the component details for the components covered in this chapter.

Table 11-1. Component Details

Name	Version	Package
DbUtils	1.0	org.apache.commons.dbutils
Codec	1.2	org.apache.commons.codec
JXPath	1.1	org.apache.commons.jxpath
Discovery	0.2	org.apache.commons.discovery

I will begin with DbUtils, a component that has recently moved into the Commons Proper. My first reaction when I realized what it could do for me was, "Where were you until now?"

Implementing DbUtils

JDBC code is one section of Java coding that leads to an amazing amount of repetitive code being written. To add to that, silly mistakes almost always plague JDBC code. Writing good JDBC code is not difficult but can be quite painful at times.

The DbUtils component is a nice, simple component that does nothing complex but just makes many JDBC tasks a shade easier for the developer. Although many persistence frameworks and packages are available these days that aim at making data persistence a little easier, JDBC still is very much the bread and butter for most Java and Java 2 Enterprise Edition (J2EE) developers. So anything that makes working with JDBC easier is good news.

You can download DbUtils from `http://jakarta.apache.org/commons/dbutils/`.
It does not depend on any other Commons component and only expects the following:

- Java Development Kit (JDK) 1.2 (or later)

- JDBC 2.0 (or later)

The DbUtils documentation is not the best around but is enough to get you
going. In the next section, you will see the most useful classes in DbUtils and
some examples of their usage. You should be able to quite easily use the code in
this chapter and start using DbUtils on your project right away. I will focus on
two classes (`org.apache.commons.dbutils.DbUtils` and `org.apache.commons.dbutils.`
`QueryRunner`) and one interface (`org.apache.commons.dbutils.ResultSetHandler`).
Before you see examples of their usage, you will zoom in a little closer and check
out what they offer.

DbUtils

`DbUtils` is a class that provides utility methods; these methods perform routine
tasks such as closing connections and loading JDBC drivers. All the methods
are static.

The important methods in this class are as follows:

close: The `DbUtils` class provides three overloaded `close` methods. These
methods check if the parameter provided is null, and if it is not, they
close a `Connection`, `Statement`, and `ResultSet`.

closeQuietly: The `closeQuietly` method not only avoids closing if the
`Connection`, `Statement`, or `ResultSet` is null but also hides any `SQLException`
that is thrown in the process. This is useful if you do not intend to handle
the exception. Of the overloaded `closeQuietly` methods, a particularly
useful one is `closeQuietly(Connection conn, Statement stmt, ResultSet`
`rs)` because in most cases `Connection`, `Statement`, and `ResultSet` are the
three things you use and have to close in the `finally` block. Using this
method, your `finally` block can have just this one method invocation.

commitAndCloseQuietly(Connection conn): This method commits the
`Connection` and then closes it without escalating any `SQLException` that
might occur in the process of closing.

loadDriver(String driverClassName): This method loads and registers the JDBC driver and returns `true` if it succeeds. Using this method you do not need to handle a `ClassNotFoundException`. Using the `loadDriver` method, the code gets easier to understand and you also get a useful boolean return value that tells you whether the driver class was loaded.

ResultSetHandler

As the name suggests, implementations of this interface handle a `java.sql.ResultSet` and can convert and manipulate data into any form you want that is useful for the application and easier to use. The component provides the `ArrayHandler`, `ArrayListHandler`, `BeanHandler`, `BeanListHandler`, `MapHandler`, `MapListHandler`, and `ScalarHandler` implementations.

The `ResultSetHandler` interface provides a single method: `Object handle(java.sql.ResultSet rs)`. So any `ResultSetHandler` implementation takes a `ResultSet` as input, processes it, and returns an object. Because the return type is `java.lang.Object`, apart from not being able to return Java primitives, there is no restriction on what can be returned. If you find that none of the seven implementations provided serves your purpose, you can always write and use your own implementation.

QueryRunner

This class simplifies executing SQL queries. It takes care of many of the mundane tasks involved and, in tandem with `ResultSetHandler`, can drastically cut down on the code that you need to write. The `QueryRunner` class provides two constructors. One is an empty constructor, and the other takes a `javax.sql.DataSource` as a parameter. So in cases where you do not provide a database connection as a parameter to a method, the `DataSource` provided to the constructor is used to fetch a new connection and proceed.

The important methods in this class are as follows:

query(Connection conn, String sql, Object[] params, ResultSetHandler rsh): This method executes a select query where the values in the `Object` array are used as replacement parameters for the query. The method internally handles the creation and closure of a `PreparedStatement` and the `ResultSet`. The `ResultSetHandler` is responsible for converting the data from the `ResultSet` into an easier or application-specific format to use.

query(String sql, Object[] params, ResultSetHandler rsh): This is almost the same as the first method; the only difference is that the connection is not provided to the method and is retrieved from the DataSource provided to the constructor or is set using the setDataSource method.

query(Connection conn, String sql, ResultSetHandler rsh): This executes a select query that expects no parameters.

update(Connection conn, String sql, Object[params): This method is used to execute an insert, update, or delete statement. The Object array holds the replacement parameters for the statement.

You will now see an example where you will fetch some data from a database. For the example, I am using a MySQL database that you can freely download from http://www.mysql.com/. You will also need to download the MySQL JDBC driver from http://www.mysql.com/. The MySQL database is running on localhost port 3306. The database name is test. The table you will be using has the structure shown in Table 11-2.

Table 11-2. Student *Table*

Columns	Type
StudId	int
Name	varchar

In Listing 11-1, you will fetch data from the Student table and modify it to suit your needs. Although you are using JDBC, note that you hardly write any JDBC code. (You might have to change the database details stated in the example based on your specific database configuration.)

Listing 11-1. UseDbUtils

```
package com.commonsbook.chap11;
import org.apache.commons.dbutils.*;
import org.apache.commons.dbutils.handlers.*;

import java.sql.Connection;
import java.sql.DriverManager;
import java.sql.SQLException;

import java.util.List;
import java.util.Map;
```

```java
public class UseDbUtils {
    public static void main(String[] args) {
        Connection conn = null;
        String jdbcURL = "jdbc:mysql://127.0.0.1:3306/test";
        String jdbcDriver = "com.mysql.jdbc.Driver";

        try {
            DbUtils.loadDriver(jdbcDriver);
            //Username "root". Password ""
            conn = DriverManager.getConnection(jdbcURL, "root", "");

            QueryRunner qRunner = new QueryRunner();
            System.out.println("***Using MapListHandler***");

            List lMap = (List) qRunner.query(conn,
                    "SELECT StudId, Name FROM Student WHERE StudId IN (?, ?)",
                    new String[] { "1", "2" }, new MapListHandler());

            for (int i = 0; i < lMap.size(); i++) {
                Map vals = (Map) lMap.get(i);

                System.out.println("\tId >>" + vals.get("studid"));
                System.out.println("\tName >>" + vals.get("name"));
            }

            System.out.println("***Using BeanListHandler***");

            List lBeans = (List) qRunner.query(conn,
                    "SELECT StudId, Name FROM Student",
                    new BeanListHandler(StudentBean.class));

            for (int i = 0; i < lBeans.size(); i++) {
                StudentBean vals = (StudentBean) lBeans.get(i);

                System.out.println("\tId >>" + vals.getStudId());
                System.out.println("\tName >>" + vals.getName());
            }
        } catch (SQLException ex) {
            ex.printStackTrace();
        } finally {
            DbUtils.closeQuietly(conn);
        }
    }
}
```

This code takes the following steps:

1. Load the JDBC Driver class, and get a database connection using the DriverManager.

2. Instantiate the QueryRunner class.

3. Use the query method that takes the connection, SQL query, parameters, and the ResultSetHandler as input. You use an org.apache.commons. dbutils.handlers.MapListHandler. A MapListHandler takes a ResultSet and returns a java.util.List of java.util.Map instances. So every row in the ResultSet becomes a java.util.Map, and all these java.util.Map instances are held together in a java.util.List.

4. Iterate through the List while picking values from each Map in the List.

5. Use the QueryRunner to execute a method that takes no parameters. Here you use the BeanListHandler, which is a particularly useful ResultSetHandler because you can convert the ResultSet into a List of a specific bean. Here you specify the bean class to be StudentBean, as shown in Listing 11-2.

6. You iterate through the List of beans retrieved and pick values from each instance of StudentBean.

Listing 11-2. StudentBean

```
package com.commonsbook.chap11;
public class StudentBean {
    public int studId;
    public String name;

    public StudentBean() {
    }

    public void setName(String name) {
        this.name = name;
    }

    public String getName() {
        return name;
    }

    public void setStudId(int studId) {
```

```
        this.studId = studId;
    }

    public int getStudId() {
        return studId;
    }
}
```

 NOTE StudId *in the* StudentBean *class had to be* int *because the type of the* StudId *column in the* Student *table is* int. *Adhering to this type matching is the only rule that needs to be followed.*

Because in this case the properties of the StudentBean class and the fields of the table Student mapped perfectly, just specifying the StudentBean class as a parameter did the trick. The field values got inserted into properties with the same name as the field names. However, if you want more control over the creation of the bean, the BeanListHandler class provides a second constructor: BeanListHandler(java.lang.Class type, RowProcessor convert). Implementations of the RowProcessor interface convert rows in the ResultSet into objects. In the StudentBean case, the BasicRowProcessor implementation of RowProcessor was used and was capable of handling the task. However, you can write a new implementation and provide that to the BeanListHandler constructor.

The output upon executing the code is of course dependent on what data you have in the Student table. In my case, I got the following output:

```
***Using MapListHandler***
  Id >>1
  Name >>One
  Id >>2
  Name >>Two
***Using BeanListHandler***
  Id >>1
  Name >>One
  Id >>2
  Name >>Two
  Id >>3
  Name >>Three
```

You should also understand the following classes:

org.apache.commons.dbutils.QueryLoader: The QueryLoader class is a simple class that loads queries from a file into a Map. You then pick queries from the Map as and when required. Having queries in a file also makes changes easily possible without having to touch the code.

org.apache.commons.dbutils.wrappers.SqlNullCheckedResultSet: This class can be useful to have a systematic way of tackling null values. Wrap a normal ResultSet with an instance of SqlNullCheckedResultSet and then specify what should be done in case of null values.

org.apache.commons.dbutils.wrappers.StringTrimmedResultSet: Wrap a ResultSet with StringTrimmedResultSet so you can trim all strings returned by the getString() and getObject() methods.

Thus, although the DbUtils component is nice and small, it does pack quite a punch and is well worth adopting on all projects where you use JDBC.

Implementing Codec

Codec is a component that provides implementations for encoders and decoders for common encoding schemes such as Base64, Hex, and Uniform Resource Locator (URL) encoding. This component consists of the following packages:

org.apache.commons.codec: The important contents of this package are the interfaces that are implemented by specific encoders and decoders in the other packages.

org.apache.commons.codec.binary: This package has the class Base64, which provides encode and decode methods for Base64. Besides being used for encoding email attachments, Base64 is used for basic authentication on Web sites. So you would have to encode a username and password using Base64 to successfully be authenticated on such sites. However, Base64 is no substitute for encryption, and Base64-encoded messages can be quite easily decoded. The class Hex provides Hex encoding and decoding capabilities.

org.apache.commons.codec.digest: This package has the single class DigestUtils that provides static methods to work with java.security. MessageDigest tasks.

org.apache.commons.codec.language: This package provides the language and phonetic encoders DoubleMetaphone, Metaphone, RefinedSoundex, and Soundex.

org.apache.commons.codec.net: This package has the class URLCodec that implements the www-form-urlencoded encoding scheme. This encoding is the reason why the URLs you often see in the browser's address box seem so strange. With this encoding, a slash (/) becomes %2F, an ampersand (&) becomes %26, and a right bracket (}) becomes %7D.

You can download the Codec component from http://jakarta.apache.org/commons/codec/.

Implementing JXPath

The JXPath component provides an interpreter for the XML Path Language (XPath). XPath is normally used in Extensible Stylesheet Language (XSL) to refer to specific tags and attributes in an Extensible Markup Language (XML) document. XPath is quite good at doing this, and a proper XPath expression can easily fetch you a value from anywhere in an XML file. JXPath takes this idea of XPath further so that XPath-like expressions can be used to get and set values even from JavaBeans, maps, servlet contexts, and so on.

The JXPath home page is at http://jakarta.apache.org/commons/jxpath/. The JXPath documentation is good, and a proper user guide is provided. XPath knowledge is not a prerequisite to start using JXPath, but XPath knowledge will make using JXPath a little easier. I suggest you visit http://www.w3schools.com/ for a tutorial on XPath.

A JXPath Usage Example

You will now see some examples that demonstrate JXPath features. Listing 11-3 shows the various uses of JXPath to access properties in a bean.

NOTE   *I am reusing the same classes used in Chapter 7. Listing 7-5 shows the* Course *class, 7-6 shows the* Student *class, and Listing 7-8 shows the* Academy *class.*

Listing 11-3. UseJXPath

```
package com.commonsbook.chap11;
import com.commonsbook.chap7.academy.*;
import java.util.*;
import org.apache.commons.jxpath.*;

public class UseJXPath {
    String[] daysOfWeek = new String[] {
```

```
                "Monday", "Tuesday", "Wednesday", "Thursday", "Friday", "Saturday",
                "Sunday"
        };
    Map tel = new HashMap();

    public static void main(String[] args) {
        UseJXPath useJXPath = new UseJXPath();
        useJXPath.fetchValues();
    }

    public void fetchValues() {
        Course course = new Course();
        JXPathContext courseCtx = JXPathContext.newContext(course);

        //Set Course name
        courseCtx.setValue("name", "A Course");

        Student student = new Student();
        JXPathContext studentCtx = JXPathContext.newContext(student);

        Vector courses = new Vector();
        courses.add(course);

        //Set Student name and add courses to Student
        studentCtx.setValue("name", "A Student");
        studentCtx.setValue("courses", courses);

        Academy academy = new Academy();
        JXPathContext academyCtx = JXPathContext.newContext(academy);

        Vector students = new Vector();
        students.add(student);

        //Set Academy name and all students to academy.
        academyCtx.setValue("name", "An Academy");
        academyCtx.setValue("students", students);

        System.out.println("Academy name >>" + academyCtx.getValue("name"));
        System.out.println("Academy > Student name =" +
            academyCtx.getValue("students/name"));
        System.out.println("Academy > Student Course name =" +
            academyCtx.getValue("students/courses/name"));
        System.out.println("Academy > Student =" +
            academyCtx.getValue("students[1]"));
```

```
        JXPathContext thisCtx = JXPathContext.newContext(this);


        //Iterator for daysOfWeek whose index < 6
        Iterator weekDays = thisCtx.iterate("daysOfWeek[position() < 6]");


        while (weekDays.hasNext()) {
            System.out.println("Weekday =" + weekDays.next() + "\t");
        }


        //Set into HashMap. Key is home. Value is 1111
        thisCtx.setValue("tel/home", "1111");
        System.out.println("Home Tel =" + thisCtx.getValue("tel/home"));
    }

    public void setDaysOfWeek(String[] daysOfWeek) {
        this.daysOfWeek = daysOfWeek;
    }

    public String[] getDaysOfWeek() {
        return daysOfWeek;
    }

    public void setTel(Map tel) {
        this.tel = tel;
    }

    public Map getTel() {
        return tel;
    }
}
```

The method `JXPathContext.newContext` plays an important part in how the code works in Listing 11-3. Creating a `JXPathContext` is quite integral to using JXPath. You always need to create a new `JXPathContext` before you can get or set values. The output upon executing the code in Listing 11-3 is as follows:

```
Academy name >>An Academy
Academy > Student name =A Student
Academy > Student Course name =A Course
Academy > Student =
Student name>> A Student
  CourseId>>> null  CourseName>>> A Course
Weekday =Monday
Weekday =Tuesday
```

```
Weekday =Wednesday
Weekday =Thursday
Weekday =Friday
Home Tel =1111
```

In Listing 11-3, you first have to set the name property for the Course class. So you create a new instance of Course and then use that to create a new JXPathContext. Note that you are expected to use the static newContext method and not the constructor. Once you have the JXPathContext named courseCtx, you use the setValue method to set the value of the name property. The setValue method will use the setXxx methods provided by the bean in question to set the value specified. Similarly, you set the student name, student course, and academy name.

Once you have set all these values, while getting back these values, you do the interesting stuff by using expressions to fetch values. So you use the expression students/name to get the name of the student at the first position in the students' Vector present in the Academy class. The expression students/courses/name gets you the name of the first course in the courses' Vector for that student. The expression students[1] gets you the Student object at the first position in the Vector. Because you have used this call in a System.out.println, the toString method for the Student class will generate the output.

You next use JXPath's capability to get you an Iterator over some of days in the daysOfWeek array. The expression daysOfWeek[position() < 6] gets you an Iterator over only the weekdays. Lastly, you use the expression tel/home to set a value of 1111 against the key home in the HashMap named tel.

Because Jakarta is primarily about server-side Java, it is natural that JXPath also has some features meant for usage in servlets and Java Server Pages (JSPs).

JXPath for Servlets and JSPs

Servlets and JSPs are two of the most popular Java server-side technologies. If you are new to servlets and JSPs, visit http://java.sun.com/products/servlets/. The package org.apache.commons.jxpath.servlet provides JXPathContext implementations for the servlet scopes PageContext, ServletRequest, HttpSession, and ServletContext. You can use these implementations to easily pick values from request, session, application, and pageContext. You will now see some examples of servlets. Listing 11-4 shows JXPath usage in a servlet.

Listing 11-4. doGet method in the servlet JXPathServlet

```
public void doGet(HttpServletRequest request, HttpServletResponse response)
    throws ServletException, IOException {
    response.setContentType("text/html");
```

```
        PrintWriter out = response.getWriter();
        JXPathContext requestCtx = JXPathServletContexts.getRequestContext(request,
                getServletContext());
        requestCtx.setValue("testattrib", "REQ TEST VALUE");

        out.println("<html>");
        out.println("<head><title>JXPathServlet</title></head>");
        out.println("<body>");

        out.println("<p>" + requestCtx.getValue("testattrib") + "</p>");

        out.println("</body></html>");
        out.close();
}
```

Listing 11-4 shows JXPath usage in a servlet. In the doGet method, you first create a new JXPathContext for the request using this method:

```
static JXPathContext getRequestContext(ServletRequest, ServletContext)
```

You then set an attribute named testattrib into the request and then fetch that value using the getValue method. Upon executing this servlet, "REQ TEST VALUE" is displayed in the browser. You will next see in Listing 11-5 how you can use JXPath in JSPs to pick values from request, session or application scope.

Listing 11-5. JXPathTrial.jsp

```
<%@ page import="org.apache.commons.jxpath.servlet.JXPathServletContexts"
import="org.apache.commons.jxpath.JXPathContext"%>
<html>
<%
request.setAttribute("testattrib", "REQ TEST VALUE");
session.setAttribute("testattrib", "SES TEST VALUE");
application.setAttribute("testattrib", "APP TEST VALUE");
JXPathContext pageCtx= JXPathServletContexts.getPageContext(pageContext);
%>
<body>
<p><%=pageCtx.getValue("$request/testattrib")%><p>
<p><%=pageCtx.getValue("$session/testattrib")%><p>
<p><%=pageCtx.getValue("$application/testattrib")%><p>
</body>
</html>
```

Upon executing this JSP, the following is displayed in the browser:

```
REQ TEST VALUE
SES TEST VALUE
APP TEST VALUE
```

This shows that in each case the getValue method picks a value based on whether $request, $session, or $application is used. You can use any of the predefined variables: page, request, session, or application.

Now that you have quickly looked at JXPath, you will move to another interesting Commons component, Discovery.

Implementing Discovery

The Discovery component is a component that will find implementations of interfaces. If your application needs to use an implementation for a certain interface and does not care which specific implementation class is being used, using the Discovery component can help you locate an implementation for the interface and use it. Discovery can be particularly useful if you are implementing the Factory design pattern to create new objects; it can first find an implementation and then create an instance. The Discovery component depends on JDK version 1.1.8 or higher and the Commons Logging component, so you will need the Commons Logging Java Archive (JAR) file to be able to use Discovery.

You will now see a quick example where you write a new interface and two classes that implement that interface. You will then use the Discovery component to look up the classes implementing the interface. You will be simulating a scenario that you could encounter while developing applications where you have to find implementations for an interface and decide at runtime which implementation will be used.

Listing 11-6 shows an interface named Discoverable that has the single method explore.

Listing 11-6. Discoverable *Interface*

```
package com.commonsbook.chap11;
public interface Discoverable {
    public void explore();
}
```

Listing 11-7 is an implementation of the Discoverable interface. The class ExploreOne implements the method explore and prints "Exploring One" upon execution of the method.

Listing 11-7. ExploreOne *Class*

```
package com.commonsbook.chap11;
public class ExploreOne implements Discoverable {
    public void explore() {
        System.out.println("Exploring One");
    }
}
```

Listing 11-8 is another implementation of the Discoverable interface. The ExploreTwo class prints "Exploring Two" upon execution of the explore method.

Listing 11-8. ExploreTwo *Class*

```
package com.commonsbook.chap11;
public class ExploreTwo implements Discoverable {
    public void explore() {
        System.out.println("Exploring Two");
    }
}
```

You now will write a new class that will use the Discovery component to find an implementation of the Discoverable interface. Listing 11-9 shows this class. The code is pretty straightforward. You instantiate the DiscoverClass and then use the find method to find an implementation of the Discoverable interface. You then instantiate this class and invoke the method explore. Note that nowhere do you use the actual implementation classes ExploreOne and ExploreTwo. So for this client code, the interface is all that matters, and the implementation class is not a concern.

Listing 11-9. UseDiscovery *Class*

```
package com.commonsbook.chap11;
import org.apache.commons.discovery.tools.DiscoverClass;

public class UseDiscovery {
    public static void main(String[] args) throws Exception {
        DiscoverClass discoverClass = new DiscoverClass();
        Class discovered = discoverClass.find(Discoverable.class);
        System.out.println("Class >>"+discovered);
```

```
        Discoverable disc = (Discoverable) discovered.newInstance();
        disc.explore();
    }
}
```

So if you do not specify the implementing class, which implementation will actually get used? For the answer you need to look at how the find method of the DiscoverClass class works. The find method uses the first non-null value fetched from the following options:

- The value of the system property whose name is the same as the interface's fully qualified class name.

- The value of property that is provided as a parameter, whose name is the same as the interface's fully qualified class name.

- The value obtained using the JSDK1.3+ "service provider" specification. This does not mean there is a dependency on JSDK 1.3 because the specification is implemented internal to Discovery.

If all three alternatives do not return a value, you will get a DiscoveryException with the message "No implementation defined for com.commonsbook.chap11. Discoverable." You will use the Java command's -D option to specify the implementation class while executing the class UseDiscovery. So use the following Java option and execute this code:

```
-Dcom.commonsbook.chap11.Discoverable=com.commonsbook.chap11.ExploreTwo
```

The output upon execution will be as follows:

```
Class >>class com.commonsbook.chap11.ExploreTwo
Exploring Two
```

As depicted by the code, the find method picks up the implementation class specified, and the method gets invoked on an instance of ExploreTwo.

Summary

You have now worked through 11 chapters of this book and have seen more than a dozen Commons components. I have tried to cover all the components I thought would be the most useful to you. However, some other Commons components might also be useful in your applications. Visit http://jakarta.apache.org/commons/ on a regular basis to stay abreast of the dynamic technologies of the Jakarta Commons project.

Finally, the Commons mailing lists are very active, and you can expect queries to be answered in a day or two. The user list is `commons-user@jakarta.apache.org`; the developer list, which has high traffic and is where all the development discussions take place, is at `commons-dev@jakarta.apache.org`. To subscribe to the user list, just send an empty mail to `commons-user-subscribe@jakarta.apache.org`; for the developer list, send the mail to `commons-dev-subscribe@jakarta.apache.org`.

Index